WINTER 1986          VOLUME 15    NUMBER 1

# Notes on
# the Contributors

FRANCES MYRNA KAMM is Assistant Professor of Philosophy at New York University. She is the author of "Equal Treatment and Equal Chances" (*Philosophy & Public Affairs* 14, no. 2 [Spring 1985]) and is currently working on a book concerned with moral problems of harming, not aiding, and the foundations of nonconsequentialism.

JOHN MARTIN FISCHER is Associate Professor of Philosophy at Yale University. His primary fields of interest are moral philosophy, metaphysics, philosophy of religion, and philosophy of mind. He is presently editing a collection of articles by contemporary philosophers entitled *Moral Responsibility* (forthcoming, Cornell University Press).

ROBERT H. ENNIS is Professor of Philosophy of Education at the University of Illinois. He is the author of *Ordinary Logic* (Prentice-Hall, 1969) and *Logic in Teaching* (Prentice-Hall, 1969) and has published several articles on causality. Professor Ennis is currently working on a book entitled *Critical Thinking*.

SHELLY KAGAN, Assistant Professor of Philosophy at the University of Pittsburgh, is a previous contributor to *Philosophy & Public Affairs*. He is writing a book on the limits of our obligation to aid others, to be published by Oxford University Press.

JUDITH JARVIS THOMSON, a past contributor to *Philosophy & Public Affairs*, is Professor of Philosophy at MIT. Her fields of interest are moral philosophy and metaphysics.

THOMAS W. POGGE is Assistant Professor of Philosophy at Columbia University. He has written papers on Kant, Rawls, and global justice.

DONALD C. HUBIN is Associate Professor of Philosophy at The Ohio State University. His primary interests are political philosophy, ethics, and decision theory. He is currently working on a theory of practical reasons.

FRANCES MYRNA KAMM       Harming, Not Aiding,
                        and Positive Rights

There has been much philosophical discussion of the claim that killing
and letting die are morally equivalent per se (henceforth, Thesis E). There
has been some discussion of the claim that harming and not aiding when
less than life is at stake are morally equivalent per se (henceforth, Thesis
GE). In this article I shall be concerned primarily with how broad the
implications would be if these two equivalences were true. That is, I will
be concerned with what new rights people could be shown to have if
Theses E and GE were true. In particular, I shall be concerned with
whether Thesis GE can have the very radical implication that it would
be wrong to deny anyone any type of thing that it would be wrong to
take away from someone.

I will argue that there are two versions of Theses E and GE, one version
having broader implications than the other. To do this it will be necessary
to explore the notion of moral equivalence, and to discuss the methodology
of testing for it. I will further argue that even if the broad version of
Theses E and GE were true, the need to apply them to cases that are
equivalent in all respects limits the extent to which they can be used to
derive new duties to aid or claims to have things. I will also consider
some ways in which the *cases* that are typically used in the discussions

Versions of this article were presented to the New York University Law and Philosophy
Seminar (1982), the New Jersey Regional Philosophical Association meeting (November
1982), the American Philosophical Association meeting, Pacific Division (1983), and the
Society for Ethical and Legal Philosophy (1984). I am indebted to the comments of the
participants in these meetings, including my official commentators, Douglas Husak and
Lizabeth Rechtin. I am also grateful to Derek Parfit and the Editors of *Philosophy & Public
Affairs* for philosophical and editorial suggestions. Work on this article was supported by
an American Council of Learned Societies Grant and a New York University Research
Challenge Fund Grant.

of Theses E and GE differ from cases to which one might be tempted to apply the Theses, and how these differences also limit our ability to derive new duties to aid and claims to have things. Although this article is not intended to deal primarily with whether Theses E and GE are true, some of the discussion will unavoidably broach this issue.

I

Those who support Thesis E often try to demonstrate it with so-called comparable cases of killing and letting die. These are cases in which all factors besides killing and letting die (e.g., motive, intent, amount of effort required to aid or not to kill) are supposed to be held constant. Killing is identified (roughly) as someone's doing something to alter a course of events from what it would otherwise have been so that, independent of anyone else's doing something later, he causes a person's death. Letting die is identified (roughly) as someone's failing to do something which would have altered a course of events that is already leading to someone's death. The following which I call "Bathtub" (B) cases, are commonly taken to be examples of comparable cases of killing and letting die:

> (B1) I drown a child in a bathtub by pushing him down in the water. I do this in order to inherit his fortune. No great effort is involved in not drowning him.
> (B2) I see a child who through no fault of mine is drowning in a bathtub. I do not make the minute effort necessary to save him, since I want to inherit his fortune.[1]

When presented with these cases, we are supposed to judge that the particular letting die is as morally bad (or as innocuous), as wrong (or as right), as the particular killing. On the basis of this it is argued that killing and letting die are morally equivalent per se, the assumption being that only moral equals will prompt equal responses when placed in equal contexts.

1. These cases are based on ones presented by James Rachels in his article "Active and Passive Euthanasia," reprinted in *Killing and Letting Die*, edited by Bonnie Steinbock (Englewood Cliffs, NJ: Prentice-Hall, 1980). Notice that the failure to get the child's fortune is not counted as a great sacrifice necessary to aid or refrain from killing, as the loss of a fortune from some other source, when it is to be used or foregone to save the child, would be.

Questions arise about Thesis E and the argument in its support. One is what it means to be morally equivalent per se. A second question is whether cases like (B1) and (B2) really do hold all factors constant besides killing and letting die. A third question is whether only equals in equal contexts could prompt equal responses.[2]

(i) It has not been noticed, I believe, that there are at least two different answers to the first question. In *tentative* versions, one answer is that killing and letting die are morally equivalent per se if there is no property which is both conceptually required in cases of the one but *not conceptually required* in cases of the other, and which makes the cases in which it is present morally different from cases with only the conceptual properties of the other. A second answer to the first question is that killing and letting die are morally equivalent per se if there is no property which is both conceptually required in cases of the one but *conceptually excluded from cases* of the other, and which makes the cases in which it is present morally different from the cases with only conceptual properties of the other.[3]

The first analysis implies that killing and letting die are *not* morally equivalent per se if a property which is conceptually true of one of the behaviors makes a moral difference in cases which the other behavior's conceptual properties do not make, even while the effect of the rest of the first behavior's conceptual properties is the same as those of the second behavior's conceptual properties. The second analysis implies that killing and letting die are *not* morally equivalent per se if a property which is conceptually true of one behavior but conceptually *excluded* from cases of the other makes a moral difference in cases which the conceptual properties of the contrasting behavior do not make, even while the rest of the first behavior's conceptual properties have the same effect as those of the second behavior's conceptual properties.

2. A detailed discussion of these questions, on which the present discussion is based, can be found in my paper "Killing and Letting Die: Methodology and Substance," *Pacific Philosophical Quarterly* (Winter 1983), and in my thesis "Problems in the Morality of Killing and Letting Die," (MIT, 1980).

3. An even stricter notion of moral equivalence (which usually lies behind the ones I have described) requires that conceptual properties of one term do not produce a different moral outcome from the conceptual properties of the other term *because* there is no difference in the role that these conceptual properties play. This is in contrast to the conceptual properties of one term having moral effects that differ from the effects of the conceptual properties of the other term but the outcomes being the same because, in effect, there are different but functionally equivalent routes to the same moral outcome.

The first analysis of moral equivalence implies that killing and letting die could be nonequivalent per se even if a *case* of killing does not differ morally from a *case* of letting die, because, for example, the case of killing contains a property which is conceptually true of letting die but not of killing. (That is, the conceptual property is "exportable.") The second analysis however requires for inequivalence that, for example, some conceptual property of killing which could not be present in a case of letting die (a nonexportable property), make a moral difference between killing and letting-die cases.

(ii) These two different analyses of "morally equivalent per se" (about which I shall say more below) go along with two different answers to the second question, about what makes killing and letting-die cases "comparable" ones for purposes of testing whether killing is morally equivalent to letting die per se. They also go along with different views of how broad the implications of Thesis E would be.

As already indicated, given the first analysis of moral equivalence per se, it might be possible to construct a *case* of killing which had morally significant conceptual properties of letting die in it, and which provided, therefore, *an instance of* killing which was morally equivalent to *an instance of* letting die, even though killing and letting die differed morally per se. For example, it seems to be *conceptually* true of my letting die (though not of my killing) that the person I let die loses out on life he would have had via my aid.[4] We could construct a killing *case* which had this property, even though the property is not conceptually true of killing. For example, I kill (directly stab) someone who is already receiving life-saving aid from me. This *case* of killing may be morally equivalent to letting the person die, other things being equal (at least when I did not interfere with someone else helping him to begin with who would have continued to help him), and may be more acceptable than killing someone in a second case otherwise the same except that the conceptual property of letting die is missing (that is, killing someone who is imposing on me the same loss I suffer in aiding, but who never needed my aid and does not need my aid, and who in being killed would lose more than life he

4. I assume that refraining from killing someone is not always construable as aiding him, so if I kill someone he does not necessarily lose only what he would have had thanks to my "aid" of not killing him. Notice that "losing out on (*only*, no more than) life he would have had if I had aided" is not the same as "losing out on life he would have had *only* via my aid." The former is consistent with several people being able to but refusing to aid, the latter is not.

gets from my aid). The conceptual property of letting die seems to make the killing more acceptable, easier to justify than simple self-defense against someone who imposes on me but stands to lose *more* than the benefit of the imposition.[5]

Notice that the conceptual distinction between killing and letting die focused on in these examples is not that between action and omission, or interference and noninterference, since action and interference occur in both cases of killing. Rather the conceptual characteristic of letting die thought to be morally significant, and so introduced into one case of killing, is that the person who dies loses only a life he would have had via the aid of the agent in question (killer or non-aider) rather than independently of his aid.[6]

If my killing someone who was already dependent on me for life support and my letting him die to begin with were morally equivalent cases, the *second* analysis of moral equivalence per se, unlike the first, would claim that killing and letting die *were* morally equivalent per se.[7] According to the *first* analysis, the equivalence of the cases would mean that killing and letting die were *not* morally equivalent per se, in part since letting die had a conceptual property that killing per se lacks which alters the moral status of cases.

Another characteristic that may seem to be conceptually true of letting die is that the person who would have to aid is being imposed on first at the time when aid is necessary by the person who needs aid. Killing in self-defense also involves someone avoiding an imposition on him that comes before he has imposed on another. Non-self-defense killings do not have this property. Suppose killing in self-defense (or on behalf of someone's defense) is easier to justify than killing someone who is not

5. I use "benefit" here in the sense of improvement over the state the person would otherwise have been in without the imposition.

6. Abortion might be construed as a case of killing which shares a conceptual property of letting die, and in which a killing is almost as permissible as a letting die. That is, a case in which someone being killed loses only life he would have had via someone's aid. I have discussed the abortion case and the problems with such an analysis in "The Problem of Abortion," in *Ethics for Modern Life*, eds. Abelson & Friquenon (New York: St. Martin's Press, 1982). When I speak of introducing a conceptual property of letting die into a case of killing, I do not mean merely describing the case so that the killer *also* lets his victim die, as when a killer stands by and watches his victim bleed to death when he could still save him.

7. I believe this is the way Bruce Russell argues in "Presumption, Intrinsic Relevance, and Equivalence," *Journal of Medicine and Philosophy* 4: 263–68.

first imposing (other things being equal including the losses one or the person would suffer if one did not do the act that kills). This might be taken to indicate that letting die has another conceptual property which contributes (at least when the loss to be suffered in aiding is sufficiently high and there is no prior first imposition by the non-aider on the person he does not aid) to its being per se morally less offensive than killing.

If we used the first analysis of moral equivalence, therefore, we would not construct comparable killing and letting-die cases by introducing factors that were conceptually true of killing or letting die into cases of the contrasting behavior. (That is, we would not "cross-conceptually," or as I put it, "cross-definitionally (CD-) equalize" factors.) If certain conceptual properties had differential moral significance, equalizing for them would only *conceal* the real moral differences between killing and letting die per se by compensating for the absence of morally significant conceptual properties. On the other hand, if, for example, none of the conceptual properties of letting die differed in moral significance from those of killing, there would be no effect in not equalizing for them. Therefore, if we adopt the first notion of equivalence, we should construct comparable cases by equalizing cases *only for factors outside the* definitions of killing or letting die (e.g., motive, intention, efforts involved). That is, we should only, as I put it, "contextually (or C-) equalize." (As I shall use these terms, CD-equalized cases need to be *also* C-equalized, but C-equalized cases are *only* C-equalized.)

By contrast, if we used the second analysis of moral equivalence, we *would* CD-equalize to produce comparable cases, since only in this way could we see if there is moral significance in properties that *must* distinguish cases of killing from cases of letting die (e.g., conceptual properties true of killing which *no case* of letting die could have, properties which cannot be *exported* into a letting die case).

So according to the first analysis of moral equivalence, (B1) and (B2) are comparable killing and letting-die cases if they are indeed C-equalized. According to the second analysis, they are not comparable since the killing case could be made more like the letting-die case, while still remaining a killing (that is, it could be CD-equalized). For example, it could involve drowning a child whose life I was already saving from another threat.

(iii) It is important to note, however, that if the first analysis of moral equivalence rules out the use of CD-equalized killing and letting-die cases

as comparable test cases to see if killing and letting die are morally
equivalent per se, it does suggest another use for CD-equalized cases in
a new test for the moral equivalence or inequivalence of killing and letting
die: Instead of merely comparing killing and letting-die cases, we compare
*C-equalized killing* cases with *CD-equalized* (relative to cases of letting
die) *killing* cases. If the CD-killing case is morally less offensive than the
C-killing case, it might be suggested that this shows that a conceptual
property of letting die which is not a conceptual property of killing contributes to moral inoffensiveness. If letting die per se has no other properties making it more offensive than killing, it would have at least one
more point in its favor than killing, and so differ morally per se. Therefore,
in making a killing *case* morally more like a letting-die case, we could
collect evidence for the moral inequivalence of killing and letting die per
se. Likewise we could compare a letting-die case containing a definitional
property of killing with a letting-die case lacking the property. A possible
candidate is "actively bringing about a threatening situation." Suppose I
do an act that endangers my life only because I depended on my bodyguard's promise to rescue me if I was in trouble. In this case if my
bodyguard does not aid he will have done something [promise to aid me]
which brings about an event that will cause my death when I would
otherwise have been under no threat to my life. If my having his promise
also led me to turn away others who would have saved me, he does
something that contributes to the removal of other barriers to my death
[on the model of someone's removing a victim's fire-protectant clothing
in the midst of a fire]. If not aiding in these cases, which might be said
to be CD-equalized for a property conceptually true of killing, is worse
than letting-die cases without this special property, then it would be taken
by the first notion of moral equivalence to be evidence that killing is
morally worse than letting die per se.

However, a problem arises for this new procedure, which also bears
on the tentative definition given above (p. 5) of the first notion of moral
equivalence: A conceptual property of one term could make a morally
significant difference when "exported" into a case involving another term
without having that same effect on its "homeground." For example, it
might play a purely definitional role on its homeground (making the term
what it is) with no moral significance. (We could not test for this possibility simply by removing the conceptual property and seeing if the
moral character of, for example, letting-die cases remained the same,

since removing a definitional property would make it not a letting-die case at all.) In general, a property's role may differ with its context. I refer to this as the Principle of Contextual Interaction. But in order for two terms (for example, killing and letting die) to differ per se morally, it seems crucial that a conceptual component make *a moral difference on its homeground*, not just when it is exported.

We shall, therefore, have to revise the first account of moral equivalence, at least so that killing and letting die are said to be morally equivalent per se if there is no property which is conceptually required in cases of the one, but not the other, and which alters the moral outcome *on its homeground* differently from the way that conceptual properties of the other term do on their homeground. (Once we become aware of the possibility that the *same* conceptual property might have a different effect on the outcome in different surroundings we might even do without the reference to "conceptual properties of one term that are not conceptual properties of the other," since if the *same* property had different homeground effects on the outcome this could also make for a morally significant difference between behaviors. I shall omit this fine point.)

If we do face the problem of bridging the gap between finding that a property has a morally significant role when exported and using this as evidence for its homeground role, the new technique of comparing C- and CD-equalized kill (or let-die) cases cannot *mechanically* help us decide whether killing and letting die are morally (in)equivalent. It can suggest which properties are important, but we may just have to *see* that they play a homeground role.

It is possible that the method of comparing CD- and C-equalized killing cases could still help us in another way. If, for example, the CD-equalized killing case in which we kill someone who is already receiving our life-sustaining aid is seen to be *no better* than letting someone die to begin with, but better than a killing case only C-equalized with letting someone die to begin with, perhaps we can conclude (by transitivity) that the letting die is better than the merely C-equalized killing. We may not be able to tell by this test which of its conceptual properties make it better, but won't we have reason to believe it is better?[8]

8. A problem arises for this as a *mechanical* procedure if transitivity fails to hold, that is, if act x were no better than act y, and were better than z, yet y failed to be better than z. In fact, I believe there may be particular relations between acts that make transitivity fail. For example, suppose it is equally good to give to charity A (act x) or to charity B (act y). It is also morally better to give to charity A than to charity C (act z). Still it is possible that

(iv) For now, let us put aside CD-equalized killing cases and the possibility that killing and letting die are not morally equivalent per se. That
is, suppose we accept the first analysis of moral equivalence, use cases
like (B1) and (B2) as comparable kill/let-die cases, and conclude from
them that killing and letting die are morally equivalent per se. The implications of this conclusion will be much more significant than the same
conclusion reached by using the second analysis of moral equivalence
and comparable killing and letting-die cases that are CD-equalized for
definitional properties. This is because if there is per se moral equivalence
of the first type, then this means that *no* conceptual properties of letting
die differ in moral significance from conceptual properties of killing. This
suggests that there will be more types of cases in which *a* killing and *a*
letting die will be morally equivalent; there will be C-equalized as well
as CD-equalized cases. For example, letting-die cases will be morally
equivalent to C-equalized cases in which we kill someone who would
have lived independently of our aid, as well as cases in which we kill
someone whose life we were already saving. A conclusion for per se moral
equivalence which used the second analysis of moral equivalence, in
contrast, could be compatible with the conclusion that (B1) and (B2) are
not morally equivalent instances of killing and letting die. Killing and
letting die would be morally equivalent in a smaller number of cases.[9]

We must, however, be wary of the nonobvious possibility that even
terms (and the behaviors to which they refer) that fulfill the strong first
notion of per se moral equivalence may have different effects in some
contexts: Mightn't a conceptual property, unique to one of the terms,

---

it is worse to give to charity B than to charity C. This might be because charity B is a
descendent of charity C, and it would be a slap in the face to give the offspring money
before giving to the parent. It is only if the choice between B and C is made so as to favor
B, but not if the choice is made between A and C, that this insult will occur. I have discussed
intransitivities of this sort in greater detail in my paper "Supererogation and Obligation,"
*The Journal of Philosophy* (March 1985). In that paper I said that "ought to do _____
rather than _____" and "better than" are intransitive relations. This may be too strong a
claim, since intransitivities involving these relations may be explained not by the relations
per se being intransitive, but by a particular relation between certain variables.

9. Those who support the moral equivalence of killing and letting die per se seem to
appeal to the equivalence of killing and letting die in *both* C- and CD-equalized killing and
letting-die cases. For example, Bruce Russell cites killing and letting-die cases which are
only C-equalized in "On the Relative Strictness of Positive and Negative Duties," reprinted
in *Killing and Letting Die*, pp. 215–31, and CD-equalized ones in his "Presumption, Intrinsic
Relevance, and Equivalence." I believe the original supporters of Thesis E (such as Rachels)
want cases that are only C-equalized (like B1 and B2) to also be morally equivalent instances
of killing and letting die.

which *in itself* had no moral significance interact in some cases with a contextual factor to produce a moral difference? Then whether we kill or let die could *make* a moral difference without these two *being* morally different per se. Analogously, even if there is no moral difference between chocolate and vanilla, everybody's preferring chocolate might make it wrong to buy vanilla. (I suspect that only such contextual factors as people's attitudes, desires, or beliefs could make features intrinsically of no moral significance have different moral effects.)

(v) The other side to the greater significance of the first notion of equivalence is the *reduced* significance of its corresponding notion of *in*equivalence. That is, killing and letting die would be morally different per se if any conceptual property of one made a difference on its home-ground that properties of the other didn't, even if it was a property for which a case involving the contrasting behavior could be equalized. This implies (as we have seen above) that CD-equalized killing and letting-die cases could be very close morally (perhaps even equivalent if only exportable definitional properties of each made a difference), even though killing and letting die differ morally per se. The difference per se might make no difference in these cases.

This bears on the third question with which we began: Would only moral equals produce equal responses in equal contexts? One way in which unequals may yield equal results in the same context is if the equal context involves CD-equalization of morally significant properties. But it is important to note that unequals may also produce equal responses in different ways. First, as suggested by the Principle of Contextual Interaction, the different moral significance of conceptual properties may be totally cancelled (not merely overridden) in some contexts. For example, if a person desires to die and it is in his interest to die, it may make no difference whether we kill him or let him die. (If he desires to be killed rather than left to die, it may be better to kill him than to let him die.) If we have a right to see to it that an aggressor dies, it may also not matter if we kill him or let him die.[10]

10. Just as the effect of properties may be cancelled, so may they be multiplied by special contexts. For example, I believe it is commonly thought that the seriousness of harming someone by or in the course of invading his property is more than the sum of harming him and invading his property taken separately. The seriousness of each act is multiplied to some degree by the other. G. E. Moore discusses the way a whole may be more than the sum of its parts. He calls it the principle of organic wholes. He denies however, that the intrinsic value of a part may change because of its context. See *Principia Ethica* (Cambridge: Cambridge University Press, 1903), pp. 27–36.

Two factors might interact with one context in the same way, yet the
factors might interact differently with a changed context, thus showing
that the factors were not morally equivalent per se. For example, when
the costs needed to aid or not kill are low, a killing and a letting die might
be equally wrong, but when we equally raise the cost required to avoid
killing and to avoid letting die, we might find that a killing is worse than
a letting die. Cases like (B1) and (B2) are commonly taken to be examples
of the former situation. For an example of the latter situation, suppose a
trolley is headed toward one person and the only way I can save him is
to redirect the trolley so that it kills me. It is plausible to claim that I may
let the person die. But suppose the trolley is headed toward me and the
only way to save myself is to redirect the trolley with the foreseen consequence that it will kill another person. It is less plausible to claim that
I may do what will kill the person to save my life. Letting die *needed* to
be avoidable at little cost to seem wrong, killing didn't.[11]

11. But note that Bruce Russell in "On the Relative Strictness of Positive and Negative
Duties" offers an explanation of why costs requirable to avoid killing may sometimes be
higher than costs requirable to aid, consistent with the moral equivalence per se of killing
and letting die. He argues that the total cost (that is, cost x number of occasions on which
it is expended) we could be required to incur to avoid killing and letting die is the same.
There are, however, many more cases in which my incurring a moderate cost could save
someone's life than in which it could help me avoid killing someone. (This is an empirical
fact.) If I had a duty to save all these lives, however, the cost to me would go above the
total cost that is required of me to save life *or* avoid killing. If I cannot be required to help
all those I could help, I cannot be *required* to help any at moderate cost (an implication of
a universalization procedure). Therefore, Russell concludes, I may have a duty to avoid
killing at some cost which I am not required to incur rather than let die, even if killing
and letting die are per se morally equivalent. I am not convinced by Russell's explanation,
since it seems to have the following two implications: (1) If there were very few people
who could be saved by my large sacrifice, I might have to make this sacrifice, if I had to
make the sacrifice rather than do an act which I foresee will kill someone. (2) If the combined
cost to avoid killing five actual people were more than the total cost that could be demanded
of me, I could not be *required* to incur one fifth of that cost to avoid killing one of the
people. Both these implications seem unacceptable. Since writing this article I have read
an explanation Joel Feinberg offers in *Harm to Others* (Oxford: Oxford University Press,
1984) for requiring an individual to pay greater costs to avoid killing than to save someone's
life consistent with the per se moral equivalence of killing and letting die (p. 170). He
argues that (1) *as a society* we do incur large costs to save life, as we do to avoid destroying
it, and (2) it makes sense to make saving life a function of the society as a whole and only
assign a small portion of the cost to each individual. I find at least two problems with
Feinberg's explanation: (a) the fact that society will incur large costs to save life does not
mean it should not incur even larger costs to avoid actually killing (e.g., by some social
project that would introduce poisonous chemicals into the water); (b) in cases in which
society cannot assign to individuals a *small* portion of the cost necessary to avoid a killing,
e.g., when only the person who would do the act which will kill can pay the large cost

Further, morally different factors may yield the same overall (macro) response. That is, there might be functionally equivalent but not identical routes (at the micro-level) to the same moral response. Simply equalizing for the presence of all factors besides the terms whose equivalence we are testing and getting the same responses will not ensure that the operations accounting for the equal responses are the same. (I describe this as the problem of Black Box Equalization.)[12] If the operations are different this may increase the likelihood that responses will differ in other cases with equal contexts.

Since equal responses might come even with unequal factors in equal contexts, we will not necessarily be able to predict that comparable kill and let-die cases will differ morally, even if we accept that there is a moral difference between killing and letting die per se. Sometimes our moral reasoning might seem more like a type of reasoning discussed in aesthetics.[13] We point to a factor (for example, the blue in a painting) and say it plays a role in making *this* painting beautiful, but don't therefore conclude that it will have the same effect (or any effect) in a different context. (Two alternatives to this approach might be to characterize carefully a more complicated property than killing or letting die that coincides with when killing and letting die do and don't make a difference and that will be predictive, and/or to isolate types of contexts which wipe out differences in less complicated properties.)

Even if the per se moral differences did not show up in many cases, the fact that *sometimes* killing and letting die did make a difference in virtue of conceptual properties that had a moral role in the homeground term would be enough to ground the first notion of *in*equivalence. Therefore the first notion of *equivalence* should emphasize that conceptual properties *never* have differential homeground effects. (If conceptual properties unique to each behavior and excluded from cases of the other behavior only sometimes made a moral difference this would be enough to ground the second notion of inequivalence.)

(vi) The first notion of equivalence is, therefore, very liberal in tolerating

---

necessary to avoid the act, the large cost seems to be apportioned to the individual. If killing and letting die were morally equivalent, then in situations in which a large cost for saving someone could *only* be borne by a single bystander rather than by society's agent (e.g., a fireman), why would there not be a social rule assigning the single bystander that duty?

12. In my thesis (see note 2).

13. For example, by Arnold Isenberg in "Critical Communication" reprinted in *Art and Philosophy*, ed. Kennick (New York: St. Martin's Press, 1979).

same overall responses to cases, consistent with per se inequivalence. What I believe the first notion of moral inequivalence cannot tolerate is the possibility that some conceptual property of killing has the same moral significance in some cases that a property of letting die has only in different cases. If this were so, we might still be able to speak of a moral difference between the two, but this would not imply that one was intrinsically better than the other. To retain the latter idea, and at the same time acknowledge that in some equalized cases *a* killing may even be better than *a* letting die, a proponent of the first notion of inequivalence would have to somehow distinguish the claim that special contexts cancel or make a virtue of killing's negative features from the claim that killing's features are intrinsically morally as acceptable (or unacceptable) as those of letting die.

Since one of my aims in this article is to see how far-reaching the implications of the moral equivalence of killing and letting die—and harming and not aiding—would be, for purposes of the discussion that follows I will employ the first, stronger notion of per se moral equivalence. I shall begin with the assumption that cases which are only C-equalized are the correct comparable killing and letting die-cases, and that killing and letting die in such cases are morally equivalent. In what follows I will investigate how far-reaching the implications of this stronger version of Thesis E are.

I should note that despite these assumptions, I do not in fact believe that Thesis E is correct. Rather than go into detailed reasons for my belief here, I will merely point to some general considerations. I find it hard to believe that a bystander to a harming does something as wrong in not aiding as someone who harms (in suitable C-equalized cases), since the bystander in being required to aid would be another, albeit *indirect*, victim in the situation. If *his* responsibility to help prevent harm befalling someone were as great as someone's responsibility not to harm, it would seem reasonable to conclude that the *direct victim* of harm must also do as much on his own to avoid being harmed as someone else must do to avoid harming him. But it seems to me that the potential harmer must do more to avoid harming. Furthermore, if not aiding were morally as bad as harming, it should, so to speak, be worse. This is because the person who fails to aid after an attack is the last person on whom the fate of the victim depends, and this temporal sequence might make the last of the two behaviors, if they were in themselves morally equivalent, morally worse. (It would make letting someone die equivalent to striking a second, fatal, blow after someone else has struck a first blow, necessary but not sufficient to produce death.) If Thesis E had this consequence, I would also judge it to be implausible.

## II

It might be thought that if killing and letting die are morally equivalent per se (Thesis E), then so are *harming* and *not aiding* in cases in which less than life is at stake (Thesis GE).[14] (The distinction between harming and not aiding is drawn analogously to the killing/letting-die distinction described above [p. 4].) In keeping with my treatment of Thesis E, I shall investigate the implications of a *strong* version of Thesis GE. That is, I shall assume that the claim that harming and not aiding are morally equivalent per se commits one to the view that instances of harming and not aiding in cases which are only C-equalized (as well as cases which are also CD-equalized) are morally equivalent.

The supporters of Thesis GE see it playing a part in moving us beyond Nozick's minimal state,[15] where people have strong negative rights (that is, rights not to be harmed) but weak or nonexistent positive rights (that is, rights to be aided). If it is as wrong to refuse aid as it is to harm, per se, then if people have rights not to be harmed, they will also have rights to aid (positive rights), and it may be a state's duty to provide that aid when it is needed.[16]

Philippa Foot has argued against such a form of reasoning, claiming that a case of not aiding can be morally as bad as a case of harming without this implying that there is a right to aid if there is a right not to be harmed.[17] This is because not aiding and harming can be contrary to

14. For example, Bruce Russell in "On the Relative Strictness of Positive and Negative Duties": "Given the above account of the distinction between killing and letting die, I will argue that the distinction has no moral significance in itself. . . . If the above account is broadened by replacing "killed," "dies," etc. by appropriate versions of "harmed," "is harmed," etc., an account of the distinction between harming and allowing harm will result" (p. 217).

15. Robert Nozick, *Anarchy, State, and Utopia* (New York: Basic Books, 1974).

16. Russell, p. 231, n. 24: "These considerations can form the basis of an argument for moving beyond what Robert Nozick has called 'the minimal state.' If individuals have positive as well as negative rights . . . then there is no reason the state should not protect those as well."

17. In "Euthanasia," *Philosophy & Public Affairs* 6, no. 2 (Winter 1977).

two different virtues, harming to the virtue of justice, not aiding to the virtue of charity, and only matters of justice are matters of right. Presumably this could be true even if *all* comparable cases of harming and not aiding were equally morally objectionable. (If harming and not aiding were contrary to different virtues they would be, at least to this extent, morally *in*equivalent, of course.) Evidence for a view like Foot's might be provided by the way we would treat the person who did not aid in (B2) compared to the person who killed in (B1). Could we threaten to kill the non-aider to make him aid, as we could to stop the killer from killing? If we could miraculously bring the drowned child back to life by killing the non-aider, may we do so if we may kill the killer to resurrect his victim? If we may not threaten and extract as much from the non-aider as the killer, even if we think their behavior is equally reprehensible, it may be because only the killer has violated the child's right to something. (An alternative explanation is that the non-aider violates a right the child has to aid, but violating this right is not as serious an offense as violating his right not to be killed.)

I wish to put Foot's criticism to one side in the following discussion, correct though it may be. This is because, first, even if it were not possible to derive a positive *right* from the equal moral objectionableness of harming and not aiding, it might be thought possible to derive a *duty* to aid equally as strong as a duty to refrain from harming even in the absence of a correlative right to aid. I wish to consider how far the moral equivalence theses would take us toward such duties. Secondly, it may be that some will not want to distinguish as strictly as Foot does between justice and charity, or will not want to distinguish between justice and charity in the way Foot does, and will want to derive rights so that they parallel their views on the equal moral objectionableness of harming and not aiding.

I shall now examine some ways in which one might attempt to derive positive rights or duties to aid.

## III

Those who accept Theses E and GE *might* be tempted to derive very strong *rights* (that is, ones that have negative and positive components) to have certain things or to be in certain states of well-being in the following way:

(1) Assume that Theses E and GE are correct. (2) They imply that if someone has the *right not to be harmed* by being deprived of *his* piece of property of type x, then (3) another person has the *right to be aided* in keeping or getting an instance of x. This amounts to a right to have the x. (4) If he has a right to have the x, he will presumably have a right that we not take it away. Therefore, (5) anybody can be said to have the *right to have an x*, in the sense that we must actively see to it that he has got it, and not take it away once he has it. This right to an x is *derived* from the *right to be aided*, which is, in turn, derived via Thesis GE from the right not to be harmed.

Likewise, someone might derive a strong *duty* to provide certain things in the following way:

(1)′ Assume that Theses E and GE are correct. (2)′ They imply that if someone has the duty not to harm someone else by depriving him of his piece of property of type x, then (3)′ he has the duty to aid someone else in getting or keeping an instance of x. (4)′ If he has the duty to provide the x, he will presumably have the duty not to take it away. These duties to see to it that someone has x are derived from the duty to aid someone in getting x, which is derived via Thesis GE from the duty not to harm.

I do not think this is a correct procedure for deriving rights to have things, or duties or rights to aid. (Notice, that for purposes of brevity I use "right to aid" as synonymous with "right to *be* aided" rather than with "right to give aid," and use "duty to aid" as "duty to give aid.")

The error comes in the move from (2) to (3), and (2)′ to (3)′. The move fails to distinguish between two types of situations in which we are called upon to aid: Those in which we help someone get or retain something which is his, and those in which we provide him with what is not his. A way to draw this distinction is to separate cases in which the people we would aid thereby get or keep something to which they are assumed to have a right *regardless* of whether they have a right to aid—I shall refer to this as an *independent right*—and those in which we help people get or keep something that is *not* already recognized as something to which they have such a right.

If Thesis GE is true, it only implies that not aiding someone will have the same moral status as harming someone when all factors in the harming and not-aiding cases besides harming and not aiding are the same.

All other factors may be the same when we deprive someone of *his* piece of property x and when we do not help him retain *his* piece of property x. So, if Thesis GE is true, and it is wrong to take away his x, it will be wrong not to aid him in getting or keeping his x, other things being equal. But all other factors are not equal if we deprive someone of what *is* his independently of a right to aid, but fail to help someone get what *is not* accepted as his independent of a right to aid. Therefore, we cannot show that it is wrong to refuse to help someone get some x that is *not already* accepted as his just because Thesis GE is true and it is wrong to deprive someone of some x that *is* accepted as his. "The right to have x," in the sense of the right to get it and to have it not taken away (mentioned in (5)), *cannot be derived using Thesis GE* and a claim about the right not to have things taken from us which are recognized as ours independent of a right to aid.

Likewise, the duty to help someone get an x to which he has no independent right cannot be derived using Thesis GE and a claim about the duty not to take away things recognized as belonging to someone.

To make clearer the distinction between these cases consider the following Campaign (C) cases (and also the Food cases, below p. 23):

> (C1) I arrange for $1,000 which belongs to my opponent in a political campaign to be stolen because I believe that the absence of these funds will cause him to lose the election. (I do not myself receive the $1,000.)
>
> (C2) I refuse to give my opponent the minute aid he needs to regain $1,000 of his that was accidentally left in a briefcase in another part of the state. I do this because I believe that without the $1,000 he will lose the election.
>
> (C3) I refuse to give my opponent in a political campaign the minute aid that I know he will use as seed money in order to collect $1,000 for his campaign. I do this because I believe that without the money he will lose the election.

It might seem that if Thesis GE is true, and there are no further distinctions of which to take account, then what is done in both (C3) *and* (C2) should be as bad as what is done in (C1). Some may think (C2) is not as bad as (C1). This would imply a rejection of Thesis GE (strong version). Let us ignore this for now, since I believe that there is a moral difference between (C2) and (C3) that does not depend on the falsity of Thesis E or GE. If my opponent is an ordinary politician it seems worse to refuse aid in (C2) than in (C3).

The source of this moral difference is that in (C2), but not in (C3), we help someone regain something which we recognize as his. Its being his $1,000 is not *derived* from any right he has to our minimal aid, indeed he is recognized as having a right to it regardless of whether we agree about his having any right to aid.

In general, aiding someone can involve either helping him get or keep something to which he has an independent right, or helping him get or keep something to which he does not have an independent right.[18] (C2) exemplifies the former and (C3) the latter.

Therefore, we cannot *derive* a person's right to something (e.g., $1,000), or our duty to provide it, by arguing: someone has a negative right not to be deprived of *his* $1,000, Thesis GE is true, therefore, (1) someone has a positive right to the aid, or we have the duty to provide the aid, necessary to give him $1,000 not already specified as his (when the amount of aid does not exceed the sacrifice we could be required to make rather than deprive someone of his $1,000), and (2) he has a right to $1,000 (within the limits on requireable aid).

We cannot argue in this way because there may be no right or duty to aid (via Thesis GE) unless there is first an independent right to the $1,000.

Using Thesis GE and Case (C1), we can conclude only that *a* harming and *a* not aiding are equally wrong when the $1,000 is already recognized as *his*. And, of course, if we knew that he had an independent right to the $1,000, we wouldn't need to *derive* his right to have it from the right to *aid*. If we have to *assume* that he has an independent right to something before we can *derive* his right to it, the argument for a right is circular.

I emphasize that if one only used Thesis GE and a case like (C1) to derive a right or duty to help someone get or keep *his* x, this problem would not arise. But I am suggesting that by forgetting to apply Thesis GE to cases which are properly equalized for all factors besides harming and not aiding, there may be an incorrect attempt to show that one has to help someone get something which is not independently recognized as *his*. It may, of course, be possible to prove independently of Thesis

18. The "or" is not exclusive. There may well be in-between cases. For example, suppose my opponent needed to have my minute aid to collect pledges that had been made to him. Is the money pledged his or not his, and is this case closer to (C2) or to (C3)? The point I am concerned to make is that some not-aiding cases *clearly* involve something to which someone is thought to have an independent right and some clearly do not. The fact that unclear cases exist does not mean that clear cases will not differ morally.

GE that someone has an independent right to something and then use Thesis GE to argue for the right or duty to aid to acquire that thing. The point is that this proof will have to be done; there is no shortcut via the Equivalence Theses and harming cases involving things to which someone has an independent right.

Notice also that the general point I have made is *not* dependent on my being right about that to which someone has an independent right. For example, in the Campaign cases I have assumed that I have an independent right to my minute aid, and that my opponent has an independent right to his $1,000 in (C2) but not to the $1,000 in (C3). These assumptions may be wrong, but this would not affect the general point I am making. Regardless of what we assume someone to have an independent right to, we can ask whether we can derive rights to have things or duties to give things to which there is no independent right by using Thesis GE and harming cases involving things to which there is an independent right.[19]

## IV

Now, there may well be things to which we have a claim, and which it would be wrong to deprive us of, even though strictly speaking they do not belong to us in the sense of property. These would be things that we simply "ought to have." The claim to these things differs from an independent right in that the claim seems *conceptually* connected to the idea that someone should be helped to have the things. (The independent right by itself is not in any way connected to the idea of a right or duty to aid. Notice that even someone who denied Theses E and GE could still believe that there were certain things that people simply "ought to have." He might, however, believe that the efforts required to avoid depriving people of these things is greater than the effort required to help them get it.)

The claim to these things and the claim to aid in getting and keeping them, however, is *not derived* from it being wrong to take these things away combined with Thesis GE. We simply identify a class of things that

---

19. For the most part, I believe proponents of Theses E and GE do not deny ordinary views about what one has an independent right to. Indeed they typically *use these ordinary views* about what it is wrong to take away from people (in the harming cases) in order to derive rights to aid to keep these things.

we think people ought to have, *independently* of Thesis GE. (I shall refer to such claims as *independent claims*.)

Therefore we have not used Thesis GE to *derive* rights or claims to have things not otherwise thought to be ours, or duties to provide these things, either from cases in which we have a right not to be deprived of what is ours or from cases in which we have a right not to be deprived of something "we ought to have." These results diminish the significance of the Equivalence Theses.


V

I believe that the difference between helping someone have that to which he has an independent right and that to which he has no independent right may be especially subject to oversight if Thesis GE is derived from Thesis E or adhered to against a background of attending to Thesis E. I believe that in killing and letting-die cases someone's life may be viewed as something to which he has an independent right, almost as if it were a piece of property to which he had a claim. So a case of letting die is one in which someone loses out on something to which he has an independent right. Certainly, someone's life will be something which he has already had at some point, so that saving a life will not involve providing someone with something he has never had.[20]

Insofar as there is no *letting-die* case analogous to (C3) (where (C3) involves not helping someone get that to which he has no independent right), the most that could be derived from the truth of Thesis E via Thesis GE is the moral equivalence of cases like (C1) and (C2). But if they forget that killing and letting-die cases *both* involve the question of someone retaining something to which he has an independent right, proponents of Thesis GE who are influenced by Thesis E may apply Thesis GE to a harming case in which there is an independent right and to a not-aiding case in which there is no independent right. Indeed, it may be their point to do just this, since it would be a *very* important result to use Thesis GE to *derive* rights to have new things, or duties to provide them. The implications of Thesis GE are not nearly so broad if

20. It is true that he will never have had the time alive which he will have if he is saved. But in this sense helping someone regain his $1,000 would also involve giving him something he has never had, since he will then have the $1,000 for a time period in which he has never had it before.

they are limited to helping people retain that to which they are independently recognized to have a right or claim.

To further clarify this point, consider the following three "Food" (F)
cases, which share all factors except the noted differences:

(F1) I take someone's food.
(F2) I refuse to give minimal aid to help someone regain his food which
has been lost.
(F3) I refuse to give minimal aid in order to provide someone with food
that was never his.

Suppose the food is necessary to keep the person alive, and staying
alive is viewed as something to which he has an independent claim. Then
if Thesis E were true, harming and not aiding in all three cases should
be morally equivalent.

If the food is not necessary for life, but is only a delicacy that provides
a person with pleasure, then even someone committed to Theses E and
GE should distinguish between (F2) and (F3). That is, if any of the not-
aiding cases is equivalent to the harming case (F1), it will be (F2) and
not (F3), since nothing to which someone has an independent right or
claim is involved in (F3). In fact, most people would probably balk at the
equivalence of even (F1) and (F2), and this could be evidence that Thesis
GE is false.


VI

An implication one might be tempted to draw from the distinction between helping someone get or keep that to which he has an independent
right, and helping him get or keep that to which he has no independent
right, concerns the handling of emergencies. It is sometimes thought
peculiar that more energy is spent on saving people from "crises" than
on saving people whose ordinary lives keep them in as bad a state as that
produced by a crisis. A crisis is usually an event which disrupts the
person's life as it was prior to the moment of crisis, so that aid will bring
a person back to his state before the crisis, helping him retain or regain
what he had in the past. Usually these are things to which he is also
thought to have an independent right. By contrast, aid to people who
ordinarily live in situations no better than crisis situations makes them
better off than they have ever been (or would have been without the aid);

it brings them to a state of well-being that has never and would never have been theirs.

The distinction I have drawn between the two forms of aid might be thought to account for the greater efforts made in emergencies. However, I believe it would be wrong to say that it is appropriate to make more effort in crises merely because they are cases of aiding someone in reobtaining what he already had. What is important is that he had an independent right (or claim) to what he had, but people can have independent rights to what they have never had. For example, things can be theirs, and be recognized as theirs, and yet they may not be in possession of what is theirs. This means that the urgency of putting some people in the condition they were in before a catastrophe and, perhaps would have been in but for the catastrophe, should not be greater than the urgency with which we improve the ordinary condition of others who *do* have independent rights (or claims) to things they have never had.

## VII

It might be suggested that if we could show that harming is impermissible in situations in which *no* independent right or claim is involved, then Thesis GE could be used to show that not aiding will be equally impermissible in a comparable case. This is indeed a possibility, but it will not succeed when harming *is permissible* in the absence of an independent right or claim.

To consider this issue let us examine the "Position" (P) cases:

(P1) John holds first place in his field. He has a right to the position only so long as he proves himself the best in his field, but no right to it otherwise. Jane enters in competition with him and he loses.

(P2) John holds first place in his field. Jane doesn't give him the minute aid he needs to train against competition, so he loses his position to his competitor.

Some might argue that we can only harm someone if we violate his rights in some way. If this were so, then Jane would not harm John in case (P1), since he has no independent right or claim to the position and no right not to be competed with. If Jane does not harm John in (P1), then Thesis GE could not imply that not aiding in (P2) was impermissible.

However, it seems to me that Jane has harmed John in (P1), though she did not violate his rights. This is because (roughly) if she makes someone worse off than he would otherwise have been, she harms him, and to lose a grand position one would have had is to be made worse off than one otherwise would have been. (In (P1) the person already had the position, so his losing it will also make him worse off than he was.) Nevertheless, it is not impermissible for Jane to harm in (P1), so we cannot use Thesis GE to conclude that Jane must aid in (P2).

In some cases harming may also be *worse* than not aiding even though it is not impermissible, and does not interfere with any independent rights or claims. For example, (P3) John is Jane's best friend. She wants to win race A. Though she doesn't care if there is a co-winner, she knows she will beat John. (P4) John is Jane's best friend. She wants to win race A, and is busy training for it, so she cannot help John train for his race B. She knows he will therefore lose. Putting oneself in direct competition with a friend seems worse than not aiding him, though not impermissible. If P3 is an instance of harming, then an instance of harming can be worse than an instance of not aiding, when its being worse is neither dependent on anyone's rights or claims being violated nor tied to the impermissibility of harming.

If it is sometimes permissible to harm when there is no independent right or claim to the thing lost, is it always permissible? A clue to the answer to this question comes from considering whether it is always wrong to deprive someone of something to which he has an independent right.

For example, suppose someone owns a restaurant and this gives him an independent right to it. If I enter into competition with him as a result of which he loses his restaurant, and he is worse off than he would have been, I have harmed him, and in particular harmed him because I caused him to lose something to which he *had* an independent right. I did this by causing him to lose his independent right. Yet it is (commonly thought) to be permissible to do this. So, even when an independent right to something exists, it is not true that harming will always be wrong. We could not, therefore, use Thesis GE to derive my competitor's right to have me *aid* him or my duty to aid when he is about to lose the independent right to his restaurant business through competition with someone else.

I might also permissibly do something that caused someone to lose that to which he *continued* to have an independent right. For example,

I could, by mutual consent, engage in a rope-cutting contest with my competitor during which I cut the rope that holds his restaurant to shore. (He did not consent to my doing this in particular but it was a side-effect of my doing that to which he did consent.)[21]

I could not, however, set fire to my competitor's restaurant. That is, certain means of depriving him of that to which he has an independent right are prohibited. This leads us to note that even in cases in which there is no *independent right to the thing lost*, it is *commonly thought* to be wrong to make use of certain means to get the thing away. For example, if an apple has been dropped into my lap by the wind, it seems that I have no independent right or claim to it. Yet for you to grab it away would commonly be thought to be wrong (even if I have no great need for the apple). It is thought to be wrong, however, because it is thought to violate my *right* against physical interference. Likewise, sometimes harming someone by depriving him of what is important to him (as opposed to the apple), but to which he has no independent right or claim, may be wrong only because it violates an independent right not to be physically interfered with. For example, if we grabbed away a fortune that had fallen into someone's lap.

But we do not transgress this independent right not to be physically interfered with *in* not aiding. So if Thesis E is true, it may seem that physically interfering with someone should not have significance in itself, that is, it seems that the claim that it has significance in itself is part of what Thesis E, and Thesis GE insofar as it is derived from Thesis E, must deny.

Suppose Thesis GE did entail this denial, but Thesis GE's supporters still thought it wrong to grab away something valuable that has fallen into my lap. Then Thesis GE might be taken to imply that it is equally wrong not to give someone a valuable thing to which he has no independent right or claim, at least if the costs involved in doing so are no greater than are required to avoid interference.

*Here, at last, we seem to have derived a very radical implication from Thesis GE*, one that could not be derived by using the Campaign or Food cases. It amounts to the claim that it would be wrong not to give me the same sort of thing that it would be a wrongful harm to take away by interfering with someone. For it would seem that if it is often wrong to

---

21. The distinction between losing one's right and losing that to which one has a right was emphasized to me by an Editor of *Philosophy & Public Affairs*.

grab away that to which someone has no independent right or claim, and Thesis GE is true, then we must give someone that to which he has no independent right or claim.

This apparent implication of Thesis GE is radical, since it amounts to the right to be given or the duty to give almost anything at all. I do not believe we can accept such a view. If we do not accept it, does this mean that Thesis GE (and Thesis E) are false? One route to saving Theses E and GE is to argue (1) that physical interference is not a separate negative factor when the loss at stake is life itself (or any loss much larger than interference alone), and (2) that with lesser harms where interference does indeed stand out as a separate negative factor, harming and not aiding are only morally equivalent per se when harm does *not* come about through physical interference (but through, for example, computer transfer of resources). Then the claim would be that harming someone by depriving him of something to which he has no independent right or claim without violating his independent right not to be physically interfered with (for example, by computer transfer) is not wrong and so the comparable case of not aiding is also not wrong.

This claim, however, does not seem to be true in all cases. For example, even if we factor out physical intrusion, maliciously or thoughtlessly doing what will deprive someone of a benefit to which he has no independent right or claim will often, I believe, be morally wrong.[22] If Thesis GE is true, therefore, there should be comparable cases in which refusing to give someone things to which he has no independent right or claim will be wrong, and the same effort will have to be made to provide these things as would be necessary to avoid taking them away. This means that Thesis GE has been used to derive at least some moral pressure to provide some goods to which there was no independent right or claim.

This implication, however, may be less radical than the implication derived from a refusal to factor out physical interference as a separate negative factor, since more effort may be required of us to avoid such interferences than to avoid nonintrusive harming (other things equal) and, therefore, more effort could be required to aid in comparable cases. Furthermore, many cases of nonintrusive removal of goods to which someone has no independent right or claim will be permissible, and so, likewise, should the refusal to aid in comparable cases be permissible.

22. This point was emphasized to me by Derek Parfit. He believes it is true when depriving someone of the benefit will serve neither your own nor others' interests.

Another way to retain Theses E and GE without deriving the right to be given anything it would be wrong to take from someone by physical interference, but *without* separating off interference from harming would (a) emphasize the distinction between being harmed by suffering a loss through another person's intrusion and someone's suffering the same loss without another's interference, rather than (b) emphasizing the distinction between an agent interfering with someone and not interfering. That is, someone could suffer the loss of a fortune that fell into his lap either by someone else taking it or it blowing away. (This is the distinction in (a).) He could suffer the first loss if *we* take his fortune away or if *we* do not help prevent *someone else* from taking his fortune away (do not aid him).

The version of Thesis GE which denies that physical interference counts cannot take seriously distinction (b), but it might allow for distinction (a). This would be to take the interfered-with-by-a-person/not-aided-by-a-person distinction seriously *from the victim's point of view*, but not from the actor's point of view. That is, it would be considered worse to be harmed by a person's intrusion than to be harmed by natural causes, but not worse to intrude on someone rather than to let him be intruded on.

Emphasizing the distinction in (a) would lead proponents of Thesis GE to claim that if it is impermissible to take away a fortune that has fallen into someone's lap, we must help someone against an aggressor who will take away the fortune that has fallen into his lap. Proponents of Thesis GE would not be committed to the more far-reaching conclusion that one had to help someone get a fortune to which he had no independent right or claim and that no one was taking from him. This analysis would seem to reconnect the wrongness of harming with the violation of a right. That is, not aiding, like harming, would only be wrong when the *independent right* not to be physically interfered with was being violated.

Notice, however, that such a view is in some conflict with the original analysis given of cases (B1)/(B2), (C1)/(C2), and (F1)/(F2), and further reduces the significance of Thesis GE.

For example, we shall be driven to the conclusion that intrusively taking away money in (C1) is morally equivalent only to not giving minute aid to help my opponent regain $1,000 *if someone else took it from him*, but not if he merely lost it. This further reduces the significance of Thesis

GE, since it reduces the number of cases in which a harming and not aiding are morally equivalent.

A third alternative for those supporters of Theses E and GE who do not want to abandon the Theses or accept their "radical implication" is to claim that once a person has something, he has an independent right to it, so *all* cases of depriving someone who already has something involve infringing independent rights to the object that would be lost. Then the fortune dropped into a lap by the wind is something to which the person has an independent right once it is in his lap. The fortune lying on the ground that you fail to give to someone, however, is not one to which he has an independent right. So, it being wrong to take the fortune away would not imply that it was wrong to fail to give someone a stray fortune. Such a theory of the origin of independent rights, however, seems dubious. This solution, furthermore, *would* commit proponents of Thesis GE to the view that when it is wrong to grab the fortune away from someone, it is as wrong to refuse to help someone keep such a fortune about to be blown out of his lap by the wind.

In summary, none of the alternatives to the "radical implication" of Theses E and GE seems to involve the impermissibility of harming in the absence of an independent right or claim of some sort, or the derivation via Thesis GE of a right or duty to aid in the absence of an independent right or claim. However, some new duties (or more weakly, moral pressure) to provide goods to which there was no independent right or claim do seem derivable via Thesis GE, if we either disregard interference as a negative factor per se or agree that nonintrusively depriving someone of goods to which he has no independent right or claim is sometimes wrong.

## VIII

I have considered one type of problem with deriving rights and duties from the supposed truth of Theses E and GE. I now wish to point out other problems that might arise in deriving such right and duties. Some of these problems stem from failing to apply Thesis GE to properly C-equalized cases (as explained on p. 11). This failure may sometimes be due to focusing too much on *cases* typically used in the discussion of Thesis E. Furthermore, using properly C-equalized cases may lead one to doubt the truth of Thesis GE. I shall discuss each problem only briefly, and continue to refer to the stronger version of Theses E and GE (given on p. 15).

(*1*) In the typical case of letting die (e.g., (B2)) help is needed by someone who cannot help himself, and who is not himself responsible for his predicament. But it is also possible to be called on to save the life of someone who could help himself, or even could help himself but chooses not to. Furthermore, one could be called on to aid someone who is responsible for endangering his own life. Likewise, in non-life-and-death aiding cases, I may be called on to aid someone who cannot help himself or someone who can, someone who is or is not responsible for his needing aid.

So it is a mistake to argue from the (supposed) truth of Thesis GE to the equivalence of (a) depriving someone of something, and (b) not helping someone get something which he could have gotten by himself, chose not to, and was even responsible for not having.

Yet some might be eager to use Thesis GE to argue for duties to provide people with certain things quite independently of first seeing if people could provide themselves with these things. Many demands for social rights seem to be phrased in a similar way. For example, a universal right to health care would imply that even the very rich who could afford to pay for themselves have a right to other's (or the state's) assistance. The emphasis in these proposals is on there being certain things that people should not even have to think about providing for themselves. An alternative to such a view is to have conditional rights that take the form: If you can't provide for yourself, and have not caused a loss to yourself, then you have a right to aid.[23]

(*2*) In cases typically used to convince us of the truth of Thesis E, those who harm or don't aid do so to promote bad ends, for example, the

23. The possibility that at least sometimes people should try to help themselves before acquiring a right to help from others, raises an additional point. The responsibility that people have to help themselves before relying on other's efforts does not seem matched by an equal responsibility to protect themselves from being harmed. It is the potential harmers who must carry more of the responsibility for protecting people from being harmed. In other words, a person who can, should pay the price for an improvement in his condition, but a potential harmer in C-equalized cases must pay the price to avoid making someone's condition worse than it would have been without his involvement. If this is so not merely because it is more convenient or effective for the respective first parties to watch over themselves, then it would indicate that our duties to avoid harming and not aiding in C-equalized cases differ, and that Thesis GE is wrong.

death of an innocent child in (B1) and (B2). But it is possible that those who harm and don't aid are promoting good causes or at least seeking to defeat bad ones.

For example, suppose that my political opponent is a Nazi. I should refuse to aid his bad cause, a cause of which I disapprove, at least if it is not a question of helping him to get that to which he has an independent right. It is not clear, however, that I may steal his campaign funds. In such cases, the derivation of a right to new campaign funds based on a right not to have his funds stolen seems obviously dubious. Furthermore, if we need not even help the Nazi get back funds to which he has an independent right, though we cannot take the same thing away (even by nonintrusive means), we would seem to have a counterexample to the truth of Thesis GE.[24]

(3) In cases typically used to convince us of the truth of Thesis E, the loss someone would suffer if harmed or not aided is very significant, e.g., his life. But if Thesis GE were true, then harming and not aiding should be morally equivalent even when the loss would be insignificant. However, when confronted with versions of Food cases (F1) and (F2) in which the food is a mere delicacy, it may be that the supporter of Thesis GE will want to abandon his position. This is because he may think it is sometimes wrong to take away even a trivial delicacy that belongs to someone else (that is, something to which the person has an independent right), while it is not as wrong to refuse to help someone retain a delicacy to which he also has an independent right.

(4) It is possible that those who think (B1) and (B2) are morally equivalent *assume* that there is a right to aid in (B2), and believe that the violation of a positive right is as bad as the violation of a negative right. (If they took the denial of all rights to be harms, there would no longer even be a contrast between harming and not aiding in these cases, since not aiding would be to inflict the harm of a violated right on someone.)

24. It has been suggested by an Editor of *Philosophy & Public Affairs* that the derivation of the right or duty to aid may not be more dubious in the Nazi case. It is only that how we ought to respond to the right (e.g., whether we must respect it or whether infringement is justified) differs from those cases in which bad ends are not involved. I believe that the Nazi has no right to aid, helping him get that to which he has no independent right, and I have no duty to give it. However, suppose this were not true. If the right or duty to aid would be more easily infringeable than his right not to be harmed and the duty not to harm, some distinction between the strenuousness of these rights or duties based on the distinction between harming and not aiding would still remain.

If they do make this assumption, then in other cases we could not *derive* any right to aid from a right not to be harmed and an equivalence of harming and not aiding. We would have to *independently* assume that there was a right to aid in other cases as well in order for harming and not-aiding cases to be morally equivalent.[25]

In summary, the differences between a set of cases like (B1) and (B2) and other sets to which we might try to apply Thesis GE, either cast doubt on Thesis GE itself or suggest that its implications are not as broad as might be thought.

25. In fact it does not even seem that the violation of a positive right if it exists in (B2) is as significant as the violation of a negative right in (B1), as measured by, for example, whether we would punish the non-aider as much as the killer. (See p. 17.)

JOHN MARTIN FISCHER &      Causation and Liability
ROBERT H. ENNIS

The issues we shall address are whether having caused a harm should be a necessary condition for liability for that harm, and if so, why.

Judith Jarvis Thomson describes the case of *Summers v. Tice* as follows:

> Plaintiff Summers had gone quail hunting with the two defendants, Tice and Simonson. A quail was flushed, and the defendants fired negligently in the plaintiff's direction; one shot struck the plaintiff in the eye. The defendants were equally distant from the plaintiff, and both had an unobstructed view of him. Both were using the same kind of gun and the same kind of birdshot; and it was not possible to determine which gun the pellet in the plaintiff's eye had come from. The trial court found in the plaintiff's favor, and held both defendants 'jointly and severally liable'.[1]

She then considers a hypothetical variant, *Summers II*. *Summers II* differs from *Summers v. Tice* in that "during the course of the trial, evidence suddenly becomes available which makes it as certain as empirical matters ever get to be, that the pellet lodged in plaintiff Summers' eye came from defendant Tice's gun."[2] Thomson believes that in *Summers II*, tort law yields the result which fairness requires—that Tice alone should be held liable.[3] She agrees that both Tice and Simonson acted badly. Perhaps they are equally morally blameworthy. But since Tice is responsible for

This article was conceived at the Center for Advanced Study in the Behavioral Sciences, Stanford. We are indebted in part to the National Endowment for the Humanities and the Spencer Foundation for helpful support, and wish to thank Marcia Baron for her comments on an earlier version of this paper.

1. Judith Jarvis Thomson, "Remarks on Causation and Liability," *Philosophy & Public Affairs* 13, no. 2 (Spring 1984): 102–103.

2. Ibid., pp. 104–105.

3. Ibid., p. 105.

the damage to Summers, Tice alone ought to be required to compensate Summers, according to Thomson.

Thomson's view is that liability ought to be associated with causation. This position can be contrasted with the view that "liability is to be shared among the actual harm-causer [if negligent] and anyone else (if there is anyone else) who acted as negligently toward the victim, and who nearly caused him a harm of the same kind as the actual harm-causer did."[4] On this sort of approach, which we shall call "Kantian," liability is associated (roughly) with morally bad activity (or perhaps, moral blameworthiness); and since, given their actions, it is pure chance that it was Tice's bullet (and not Simonson's) which hit Summers, both should be equally liable. Liability, the Kantian claims, should not depend on "moral luck"—it should depend on factors that are (in a suitable sense) under a person's control.[5]

Now there are many reasons not to adopt a Kantian system of tort law. A Kantian system is obviously impractical; whereas it is often possible to identify the person who has *caused* a harm, it is difficult to identify the class of people who acted equally negligently (in the relevant respect) toward the victim. Since negligence often leaves no trace, it is more difficult to isolate the pertinent class of negligent people than the class of actual harm-causers. Thus, it seems that the only feasible systems of assessing liability would be un-Kantian. Further, a mechanism for apportioning liability need not also apportion *moral* blame, and having separated the issue of determining moral blame from that of determining liability, there may be good reasons of efficiency to adopt an un-Kantian approach to liability. But we can (and we believe Thomson is willing to)

4. Ibid. Some alternative views are: 1) that liability ought to be spread among everyone, on the ground that we are our brothers' and sisters' keepers; 2) that liability for harms ought to be shared among all the people who have acted negligently; and 3) that liability for a harm ought to be shared among all who have acted negligently toward the victim, regardless of the nature of the negligence. All of the alternatives might be tempered by considerations of ability to pay.

5. Note that our use of the term "Kantian" to apply to our approach to liability is not meant to suggest that Kant would agree with all our arguments for it. The approach is Kantian at least in the sense that it insists that *moral luck* is irrelevant to liability. For interesting discussions of moral luck, see: Bernard Williams, "Moral Luck," *Proceedings of the Aristotelian Society*, supplementary volume L (1976), pp. 115-35; and Thomas Nagel, "Moral Luck," *Proceedings of the Aristotelian Society*, supplementary volume L (1976), pp. 137–51. Williams' article is reprinted in Bernard Williams, *Moral Luck* (Cambridge: Cambridge University Press, 1981). Nagel's article is reprinted in Thomas Nagel, *Mortal Questions* (Cambridge: Cambridge University Press, 1979).

distinguish the practical question from the question of what would be the "ideally" fair way of determining liability. That is, upon reflective consideration, what would be the fairest way of determining liability, apart from considerations of practicality and efficiency?[6]

Thomson has an intriguing argument in favor of her un-Kantian answer to this question. We shall divide her argument into two parts, and start with Part One. Suppose that A injured himself. That is,

(1) A caused A's injury, freely, wittingly, for purposes of his own; and no one other than A caused it, or even causally contributed to it.[7]

Now A wants to be compensated for his injury. But given that (1) is true of A's injury, A cannot legitimately exact compensation from B, according to Thomson. Allegedly B's freedom of action protects him against A's claim, and B's pockets are not open to A, no matter what we imagine about B—even that B is "playing Russian roulette on A, or throwing bricks at him."[8] In this case, according to Thomson, A may not call on anyone else for compensation—he caused his own injury.

In part two of Thomson's argument, we simply imagine that A is injured, and that B did not cause the injury. Thomson says:

Then whatever did in fact cause A's injury—whether it was A himself who caused his injury, or whether his injury was due to natural causes, or whether C or D caused it—there is nothing true of B which rules out that A's injury had the history described in (1), and therefore nothing true of B which rules out that A should bear his own costs. Everything true of B is compatible with its being the case that A's costs should lie where they fell. So there is no feature of B which marks his pockets as open to A. . . ."[9]

Thomson's total argument, then, is briefly as follows. If B's behavior is causally irrelevant to A's injury, and A freely and wittingly caused his injury to himself, then B need not compensate A because of B's freedom

6. For discussions of these issues, see, for example, Jules Coleman, "On the Moral Argument for the Fault System," *The Journal of Philosophy* 71, no. 14 (August 15, 1974); and "Corrective Justice and Wrongful Gain," *The Journal of Legal Studies* 11, no. 2 (June 1982); and Joel Feinberg, "Sua Culpa," in *Doing and Deserving* (Princeton: Princeton University Press, 1970), pp. 187–221.

7. Thomson, p. 110.

8. Ibid.

9. Ibid., pp. 110–11.

of action. And whenever B's behavior is causally irrelevant to A's injury, nothing about B rules it out that A caused his own injury. Thus, if B's behavior is causally irrelevant to A's injury, B need not compensate A. Thomson concludes that "causality matters to us, then, because if B did not cause (or even causally contribute to) A's injury, then B's freedom of action protects him against liability for A's costs."[10]

We have two different concerns about Thomson's argument for the role of causality in liability ascription, and also a concern about the alleged decisive role of freedom of action. First, it is not clear that Part One of the argument succeeds. That is, it is unclear that B is in all cases free from liability for the harm done by A to A. Suppose that both A and B took turns playing Russian roulette on A's foot. A pulled the trigger, and the barrel was empty. B pulled the trigger, and the barrel was empty, etc. Finally, A pulled the trigger, and wounded himself. In this case, B imposed a significant risk of harm to A *of the same kind as the actual harm*. When Thomson claims that B's pockets are not open to A, no matter what we imagine about B—even for example, that B was playing Russian roulette on A—her claim may gain force from a tacit assumption that the *actual* harm to A was *not* caused by (or not of the same sort as that which would have been caused by) A's engaging in Russian roulette, or whatever behavior B was by hypothesis negligently engaging in. If this assumption were made, then Thomson might be correct in saying that B's pockets would not be open to A, but this wouldn't cast doubt on the *Kantian* approach, since the example would *not* be one in which B nearly caused A a harm of the same kind as the actual harm-causer (A) did. Once it is made explicit that B was acting in a way that was *relevantly similar* to A, it is not so obvious that Thomson's claim that B need not pay some share of A's expenses is correct.[11]

Second, *even if* Part One of Thomson's argument were successful, it seems to us that Part Two fails; that is, even if Thomson's claim that B owes no compensation in the case where A causes his own injury is correct, she cannot legitimately go from this claim to a general association of causation with liability. We shall now assume, for the sake of argument, that Part One has succeeded. When (1) is true of A's injury, why might one intuitively feel that B should not be called upon to compensate A?

10. Ibid., p. 111.
11. It should be noted that Thomson is skeptical about the possibility of determining what is "relevantly similar" action (ibid., p. 105).

It is plausible to think that this intuition is based on the principle that no one is morally obligated to compensate another person who has voluntarily injured *himself.* Our moral obligations, it might be supposed, do not extend to the remedying of (at least certain) harms to another which were caused by himself. Thus, no one (including B) would be required to compensate A for A's injury, when it is self-imposed. Here, no appeal is made to any sort of principle of freedom of action. Now let us consider Thomson's crucial claim, "Then whatever did in fact cause A's injury— whether it was A himself who caused his injury, or whether his injury was due to natural causes, or whether C or D caused it—there is nothing true of B which rules out that A's injury had the history described in (1), and therefore nothing true of B which rules out that A should bear his own costs."

If C caused A's injury, nothing true of B would *entail* that A's injury did not have the history described in (1), and therefore (still supposing, for the sake of argument, that Thomson's Part One has succeeded) nothing true of B would *entail* that A should not pay his own costs. But if C caused A's injury, it may nevertheless be true that A should be compensated, and compensated (partly) by B. Let us elaborate. If C caused A's injury, then it is the case, as Thomson says, that everything true of B would be *compatible* with A's injury's having the history described in (1) and thus with A's having no claim to compensation by B. That is, suppose that C actually caused A's injury. Then there exist possible worlds in which B behaves exactly as he actually did and in which A caused his own injury, and thus (still supposing Thomson's Part One to have succeeded) in which B owes no compensation. But it would be a mistake to conclude from this fact that in the *actual* world (in which C *rather than* A caused the injury) B owes no compensation.

One way in which one could go from the fact that B's behavior is *compatible* with A's injury's being caused by himself to the conclusion that B actually owes no compensation is to assume (as Thomson appears to do) that, in order for B actually to owe compensation, his behavior considered in itself must *entail* that A should not pay all his own costs. But this seems to be an overly strong and implausible assumption. We could instead believe that B's (bad) behavior, *together with other facts which actually occur,* such as A's *not* having caused the injury, make it the case that A need not pay his own costs (and that B should contribute).

The Kantian, then, can respond to Thomson as follows. It might indeed be true that, when A caused his own injury, B need not compensate him, and this is because no one else need compensate A, since A caused his own injury. And it is clearly true that, when C caused A's injury, B's behavior is compatible with A's causing his injury, and thus is compatible with B's owing no compensation. But it does not follow that B owes no compensation. And insofar as C caused A's injury, we cannot appeal to the principle that no one is to be compensated for harm caused to himself to get B off the hook. This leaves it open to the Kantian to say that B ought to pay the same as C, insofar as his behavior was equally bad in the relevant respect.

What makes plausible Thomson's claim that, when A caused his own injury, B need not pay, is that it might seem that no one else need pay for a self-imposed injury. But it can't be concluded that *in general*, liability ought to be associated with causation. When A injures himself, it appears (still assuming the success of Thomson's Part One) that *no* compensation is owed A (and trivially, B need not compensate A). But when C injures A, compensation *is* owed A, and nothing that Thomson has said argues against the fairness of having B contribute to the compensation, if B's behavior is as bad as C's (in the relevant respect).

Finally, when C causes A's injury, can one appeal directly to B's freedom of action to protect B from having to pay compensation to A? We do not see how. Suppose that both B and C detest A, and they both (independently) shoot at A. Only C's bullet hits A. Who should pay? It doesn't seem that Thomson can appeal to B's freedom of action to yield the result that he need not pay. One could make such an argument by construing freedom of action as follows:

(2) Each person may (without penalty) engage in whatever activity he chooses, unless he *causes* injury to another person.

But why construe freedom of action in *that* way, rather than as follows?

(3) Each person may (without penalty) engage in whatever activity he chooses, unless he imposes (significant) risk of injury to another person.[12]

It doesn't seem that mere reference to our intuitive conception of freedom of action will decide the issue between (2) and (3). To insist that

12. Also, why rule out the following sort of construal?

(4) Each person may (without penalty) engage in whatever activity he chooses, unless others are in desperate need of assistance.

(2) is correct would appear to be question begging. Ultimately, in deciding whether C or both B and C should pay, one is deciding *whose* freedom of action should be curtailed (and to what extent), but a simple appeal to the notion of freedom of action doesn't settle the issue.

It might be thought that part of the motivation for choosing (2) over (3) is the difficulty of specifying what constitutes a "significant" risk in some non-*ad hoc* way. If we have enough trouble giving an account of rights against risky behavior, this alone may push us toward (2). But even if it is difficult to specify which risks are significant, we take it that it is clearly impermissible for a person to impose *certain kinds* of risks on another (without prior consent). And this is so, even if individuals do not have *rights* not to have risks imposed on them.[13] For example, you may not play Russian roulette (with a gun with six chambers) on your neighbor, and even if you do not shoot him, you do something wrong in playing the game with a loaded gun. We do not think it obviously wrong to claim that you would owe compensation to your neighbor simply in virtue of imposing such a risk on him, though this claim is not required by our position. All that is required is that you would be equally liable as someone who played a similar game and actually *did* shoot the neighbor.

We have suggested that in *Summers II* both Tice and Simonson should be considered equally liable for Summers' injury. The reason for this Kantian claim (we have suggested) is that liability should not depend on a certain kind of moral luck—on factors outside an agent's control. But consider now *Summers III*: Simonson awakens in the morning with a bad cold, and so he does not go hunting. Tice is alone when he shoots (negligently) and hits Summers. But we assume that had Simonson gone hunting, he would have acted just as negligently as Tice. (He would have behaved just as he did in *Summers I* and *Summers II*.) So, but for factors entirely outside Simonson's control (his getting a cold), he would have behaved just as badly as did Tice. But in *Summers III*, we do not believe that Simonson and Tice ought to be equally liable.[14]

13. Robert Nozick discusses this issue in *Anarchy, State, and Utopia* (New York: Basic Books, 1974), pp. 54–87.

14. Nagel considers such examples in "Moral Luck." His example is one in which a German would have acted just as badly as the Nazis had he stayed in Germany, but the man left the country before the Nazi period (say, to go into business in Brazil). Though this person is culpable on account of his bad character (or his tendencies), it seems that he is less morally reprehensible than a Nazi who actually performs atrocities. And although his character is condemnable, it seems that the German who moved to Brazil couldn't reasonably be held liable for any of the harms to the Jews caused by the Nazis.

It is hard to explain exactly why there should be this intuitive difference between *Summers II* and *Summers III*. But note that in *Summers II* all of the relevant intentions, choices, and behavior of the two persons are *the same*; it is only the consequences of the behavior that are different (as a result of factors beyond the agents' control). In *Summers III* this is *not* the case—there are different choices and behavior. We suspect that this difference will lead the way to a basis for distinguishing the kinds of moral luck operative in the two cases.

Actual choices and behavior are morally different from mere dispositions to choose and behave in a way which is parallel to the moral difference between actual and hypothetical consent. If you consented yesterday to pick me up at the airport today, then you have a moral obligation to do so. But from the fact that you *would have* consented to pick me up at the airport had I asked you yesterday, it does *not* follow that you have any such obligation.[15]

Of course, we do not claim to have established the Kantian approach in this brief article. Rather, we have pointed to what we believe are inadequacies in a very interesting argument against Kantianism. No doubt, the Kantian approach is unacceptable for practical reasons; but this leaves it open that Kantianism is the ideally fair approach.

15. Ronald Dworkin makes this point about consent in: "The Original Position," *University of Chicago Law Review* 40, no. 3 (Spring 1973):500–533.

SHELLY KAGAN

# Causation, Liability, and Internalism

Almost all of us believe that it matters who caused the damage: all things being equal, the person who did it should pay for it. If C harms A, then A has a claim against C for compensation; and C is liable *because* of the fact that he caused the harm.[1] This much seems clear. What is not at all clear is *why* causality should matter in this way. This is the sort of issue that is typically neglected by contemporary moral philosophers: secure in their intuitive judgments, they do not search for a theoretical explanation. Yet such neglect seems unjustified, for without a plausible account our confidence in this view is probably unwarranted; at the very least, our understanding of ethics will remain inadequate.

One of the most attractive features of Judith Jarvis Thomson's fascinating and suggestive article, "Remarks on Causation and Liability," is her insistence on the need for an explanation of why causality matters for liability.[2] Furthermore, Thomson herself goes on to suggest such an explanation. Unfortunately, however, her comments on this issue are somewhat obscure, in part because they are concentrated into a few difficult pages. What I want to do, therefore, is to reconstruct Thomson's argument, and see whether she has provided the necessary account.

## I

Why does causality matter for liability? Thomson takes the key to the answer to lie

---

1. On most views, causality is only necessary for liability, not sufficient. See footnote 6.
2. *Philosophy & Public Affairs* 13, no. 2 (Spring 1984): 101–133. All page references in the text are to this article. Thomson also discusses a good many other related issues in her paper.

in the value we place on freedom of action, by which I mean to include
freedom to plan on action in the future, for such ends as one chooses
for oneself. We take it that people are entitled to a certain 'moral space'
in which to assess possible ends, make choices, and then work for the
means to reach those ends (p. 108).

Presumably what this means is that a person should be morally free to
dispose of his time and resources as he sees fit—unless there is a sufficiently strong reason for morality to require him to act in a particular
way. Thomson does not explicitly note this qualification, but surely it
must be added. For all those who deny egoism must admit that some
limitations on a person's freedom of action are legitimate. Nonetheless,
it should be clear that the value of freedom of action does rule out limitations on that freedom that cannot be adequately supported. Thomson
is going to suggest, then, that the importance of freedom of action explains
why liability should be limited to those who cause harm.

Very well, suppose that A has been harmed, and he requires a certain
amount of compensation in order to be returned to the level he was at
previous to being harmed. From whom is A entitled to seek compensation? Who should pay for the damages?[3] Intuitively, of course, we believe
that the one(s) who caused the harm should be liable. But how does
freedom of action explain this?

Thomson begins by claiming that, at the very least, freedom of action
rules out the possibility that a randomly selected individual can legitimately be held liable. That is, even though A has been harmed, he is not
entitled to seek compensation from a person, X, chosen at random. Thomson's argument here is difficult to understand, however, so I want to
quote from her at some length. (I have numbered her sentences to aid
discussion.) A has been harmed, and wants to be brought back to his
previous level of well-being:

(i) But the freedom of action of other people lends weight to the following: (ii) If A wants the world changed in that (or any other) way,
then—other things being equal—A has to pay the costs, in money,
time, energy, whatever is needed, unless he can get the voluntary

3. Thomson claims (pp. 105–106) that there need not actually be a moral requirement
that the person who is liable pay the damages himself. That is, it may be morally acceptable
for a third party to pay them for him. I want to leave this point aside, however, and for
simplicity of exposition I will write as though damages should be paid by the one who is
liable.

agreement of those others to contribute to those costs. (iii) Again, A's wanting the world changed in that (or any other) way is not by itself a reason to think he may call on another person to supply him with what he needs to change it. (iv) It follows that A is not entitled to call on a person unless that person has a feature other than just that of being a person, which marks *his* pockets as open to A. (v) A cannot, then, choose a person X at random, and call on X to pay the costs— on pain of infringing X's freedom of action (p. 109).

Now the desired conclusion, of course, is expressed in (v); and as far as I can see, (iv) is intended simply as another way of stating the conclusion. If A cannot seek compensation from a person chosen at random, then he may only seek compensation from someone who is appropriately distinguished in some way—that is, someone with some particular feature by virtue of which he is legitimately held liable. Presumably the mere fact that X is able to pay and has been randomly selected is not a feature of the appropriate sort. Does Thomson's argument establish her conclusion?

Issues of fairness may cloud our assessment of the argument itself. After all, why should X be singled out for liability? His situation is not relevantly different from that of countless others. It seems to me a possible reply that if X was genuinely selected *randomly*, this somewhat mitigates the charge of unfairness. Matters would be quite different were he deliberately chosen, for example, because of his race. (Matters would also be different if, through bad luck, the random process regularly chose him.) But it might still be thought unfair that X should be liable for *all* of the damages, rather than merely a portion of them. Why shouldn't all $n$ of the people able to provide partial compensation each be held liable for $1/n$ of the damages?[4] It does seem to me that such an arrangement would be more fair; and this provides an objection against selecting a single random individual. So let us ask, instead, whether A is entitled to seek partial compensation from each X that could contribute. I take it that Thomson's conclusion is meant to rule out this possibility as well. Unless some particular feature marks X's pockets as open to A, A is not entitled to seek compensation from X—presumably not even partial compensation.

4. Collecting from all of these people might be an unfair burden to place upon A. Perhaps this could be solved by having the government—acting as the agent of the public—provide the compensation out of tax revenues.

Now as both (v) and (i) make clear, Thomson thinks that the importance of freedom of action supports this conclusion. But how exactly does it do this? The answer presumably lies in (ii) and (iii): freedom of action apparently supports these two claims, and they in turn yield the conclusion. However, since Thomson does not explicitly provide the intermediate connections, we must try to do that for her.

Obviously enough, if A *is* entitled to seek compensation from X, then X's freedom of action is more limited than it would otherwise be. *Any* moral claim against X at least partially restricts X's freedom of action (putting limits on how X may act or dispose of his resources). But, of course, the value of freedom of action does not justify a blanket rejection of purported claims against X. As I noted above, restrictions on freedom of action are justified if there are sufficiently significant reasons for them. So the question is this: is the fact that A has been harmed a sufficient reason for restricting X's freedom of action by making him liable for (partially) compensating A?

Both (ii) and (iii) answer this question in the negative. Taken on their own, all that they explicitly say is that the mere fact that A has been harmed and wants to be compensated does not entitle him to seek compensation from X. This is little more than a reassertion of the conclusion. But in context, given the suggestion in (i) that the view expressed by (ii) and (iii) is supported by freedom of action, I take it that there is a tacit appeal to the judgment that the mere fact that A is in need of compensation is not sufficiently significant to limit X's freedom of action.

If we grant Thomson's tacit judgment, her conclusion surely follows. For if A's need for compensation (and X's ability to pay) is not by itself a significant enough reason to limit X's freedom of action by making X liable to A, then someone *will* be liable (if anyone at all is) only under conditions that are more restrictive than these. That is, a person will be liable only if some particular (yet to be specified) feature marks his pockets as open.

But why should we grant Thomson's tacit judgment? We should start by noting that—although I am sure it is unintentional—Thomson may get some illegitimate intuitive mileage from the way she states (ii) and (iii). In speaking of A's desire to be returned to the level of well-being he had previous to being harmed, Thomson writes of "A's wanting the world changed in that (or any other) way." The implicit suggestion is that in evaluating the judgments made by (ii) and (iii) it is irrelevant what desire we ascribe to A. This may tempt the unwary reader into thinking that the question at issue is whether the mere fact that A desires something or the other (it doesn't matter what) is a reason to believe that A is entitled to seek the means of satisfying that desire from X. But this would be a mistake. In the issue at hand, X's freedom of action is not being restricted to satisfy any old whim of A's, but rather something more important: the desire for compensation for having been harmed.

Indeed, it might be suggested that A's desire for compensation is, strictly speaking, irrelevant. A's *entitlement* to compensation (should he desire it) has nothing to do with whether or not he actually *wants* to be compensated. Thus, the question is simply whether A's having been harmed provides a significant enough reason to justify restricting X's freedom of action by entitling A to seek partial compensation from X. Thomson's tacit judgment is that A's injury does *not* provide sufficient reason to make X liable.

Of course, even if we are clear about the precise nature of Thomson's tacit judgment, we may very well still find it intuitively acceptable. But Thomson promised to go beyond intuitive judgments—to offer a theoretical explanation that would justify the intuitions. Unfortunately, nothing in the argument we are considering offers such a theoretical justification. In effect, Thomson is saying that if we think about it we shall agree that the mere fact that A needs compensation is not enough reason to require X to help provide it. And perhaps she is right. But why *isn't* it a sufficient reason?

What we would like to have is a theoretical account explaining which considerations are significant enough to justify restricting freedom of action, which ones are not, and why. Little or no explanatory progress has been made if we merely replace our original intuition—that A is not entitled to seek compensation from X—with the new intuition—that A's need for compensation is not important enough to restrict X's freedom of action by making him liable. As Thomson herself says in another context, our "question has not been answered: we have merely been offered new language in which to ask it" (p. 108).

It is worth noting that Thomson goes on to offer an argument for the specific claim that causality is necessary for liability. (That argument will be examined beginning in Section III.) So far as I can see, however, that later argument does not presuppose the conclusion of the present argument. If it succeeds, therefore, it makes the present argument un-

necessary, for the conclusion will trivially follow: if causality is necessary
for liability, A is not entitled to seek compensation from someone unless
that person has a particular feature—namely, that he helped cause the
harm. If I am right that the present argument is little more than an appeal
to intuition, it may be just as well if Thomson can do without it.

II

Even if we grant the conclusion of the argument discussed in the last
section, Thomson has obviously not yet defended the view that causality
matters for liability. She has only shown that someone can be liable only
if he has some particular feature ("other than just that of being a person");
she has not yet told us what that feature is. It might turn out that having
caused the harm is a necessary feature for liability (as Thomson will go
on to argue), but it might not turn out that way: other features might be
sufficient for liability as well (or instead).

Thomson briefly considers the suggestion that although A may not be
entitled to seek compensation from X (the random, average person), A
may be entitled to seek it from someone who is rich. She attempts to
sidestep this issue, admitting that "freedom of action is not the only thing
we value, but I want to bring out *its* bearing on the question in hand"
(p. 109). This remark is rather puzzling. Why doesn't wealth deserve
greater attention?

Apparently Thomson sees the issue this way: Freedom of action supports limiting liability to those individuals with certain features. Since
freedom of action is not all that we value, however, there may be overriding external considerations that favor widening the circle of liability.
But it is obvious that from an internal perspective, at least—that is, one
limited to consideration of what is supported by freedom of action itself—
there is no support for the position that greater wealth is a ground for
liability.

Now it must be readily admitted that there is a sense in which freedom
of action opposes grounding liability in wealth. After all, such liability
restricts one's freedom. But in this sense, it seems that freedom of action
opposes liability on any grounds whatsoever (indeed it opposes any moral
requirements at all). All along, the question has simply been whether a
given reason is significant enough to justify a particular restriction on
an agent's freedom of action. In a sense, it seems that most such reasons

will have to be external—that is, external to freedom of action per se. But such externality is irrelevant to the question of whether the given reason is important enough to justify limiting freedom of action—and this is the only question at issue. So Thomson has no justification for putting aside the possibility that A may be entitled to seek compensation from someone by virtue of that person's greater wealth.

Perhaps Thomson had something like the following in mind: Internal to freedom of action itself is a justification for there being certain restrictions placed upon it. (For example, it is sometimes suggested that freedom of action itself supports a restriction on one's freedom to sell oneself into slavery.) Given the nature of the value of freedom of action, limitations on certain grounds have a direct and internal justification; other limitations may be justified as well, but these will be justified in terms of something *other* than freedom of action. And perhaps Thomson thinks that causation will be such an internally justifiable ground, and that it is intuitively obvious that wealth cannot be.

But all of this is mere speculation on my part. As Thomson's discussion stands, I cannot see why greater wealth should not be a legitimate, ground-level candidate as one of the features on which liability may be based. It is certainly possible, of course, that wealth does *not*, in fact, provide a basis for liability. But from the theoretical standpoint, I see no reason why the list of potential contenders for grounding liability—the list of features that need to be examined and evaluated—should not include wealth as well as causation.

Once again, it must be noted that if Thomson's later argument for the specific claim that causality is necessary for liability succeeds, then it makes the discussion of this section moot. For, trivially enough, if having caused the harm is a necessary condition for being liable, then the mere fact that someone is rich cannot itself be sufficient grounds. It is time to examine that argument.

## III

Thomson's argument that causality is necessary for liability begins by asking us to consider and evaluate cases of this sort:

> (1) A caused A's injury, freely, wittingly, for purposes of his own; and no one other than A caused it, or even causally contributed to it (p. 110).

In cases of this kind, asserts Thomson, even if A later decides that he would like to return to his previous level of well-being, he is not entitled to demand the necessary funds from another, say, B. This judgment about cases of type (1) is totally independent of what we imagine about B: "B may be vicious or virtuous, fat or thin, tall or short; none of this gives A a right to call on B's assets" (p. 110). Indeed, even if B was acting *negligently* toward A, given that A's injury satisfies (1), B is not liable for the costs of it.

We will eventually need to examine this general judgment carefully, but first let us consider the rest of Thomson's argument. Assuming that the judgment about cases of type (1) is correct, what follows?

> Let us suppose that A is injured, and that B did not cause the injury, indeed, that he in no way causally contributed to A's injury. Then whatever did in fact cause A's injury—whether it was A himself who caused his injury, or whether his injury was due entirely to natural causes, or whether C or D caused it—there is nothing true of B which rules out that A's injury had the history described in (1), and therefore nothing true of B which rules out that A should bear his own costs. Everything true of B is compatible with its being the case that A's costs should lie where they fell. So there is no feature of B which marks his pockets as open to A—A is no more entitled to call on B than he is entitled to call on any person X chosen at random (pp. 110–11).

If this is right, then Thomson has succeeded in showing that causality is necessary for liability: for if by starting with the assumption that B did not causally contribute to A's injury we can conclude that B is not liable for the costs of A's injury, then it follows that someone could be liable only if he *did* causally contribute. Once again, however, the argument in the passage quoted is a difficult one to understand. One premise, it seems to me, may be stated somewhat imprecisely; and another premise—a crucial one—seems to be missing altogether. But Thomson's argument is a powerful one for all that, and it merits careful analysis.

As I understand it, the argument as stated comes to this: (i) If B did not causally contribute to A's injury, then "everything true of B" is compatible with A's injury being of type (1). (ii) Given our general judgment about cases of type (1), however, this means that everything true of B is compatible with its being the case that A is not entitled to seek compensation from B. That is, the facts about B are compatible with B's not being liable. (iii) Therefore, B is *not* liable.

Formulated in this way, the most pressing problem is the transition from (ii) to (iii): the argument appears to move illegitimately from the modest assertion that nonliability is possible, to the bold assertion that nonliability actually obtains. If this is not simply a non sequitur, and I do not believe that it is, then something must bridge the gap. But what?

At first glance, especially in my formulation of the argument, it looks as though Thomson may be trading on an equivocation in the use of such expressions as "everything true of B," or "the facts about B," and so on. For such expressions may be taken either narrowly, including reference only to nonevaluative (descriptive, naturalistic) features, or more broadly, including reference to evaluative (normative, moral) features as well as nonevaluative ones. The transition from (ii) to (iii) is easy if we take the broad reading: for if all the facts about B—including the evaluative ones— are compatible with B's nonliability, then liability cannot be among the facts about B, and so B is not liable. However, (ii) is derived from (i), and (i) is question begging if we take the broad reading: since, by hypothesis, B is not liable in cases of type (1), to assume that the facts about B—including the evaluative ones—are compatible with the situation's being of type (1) is already to assume that B is not liable. Thus (i) should not be granted unless we take the *narrow* reading. Yet if we maintain this reading throughout, the transition from (ii) to (iii) remains problematic. This prompts the thought that the argument relies on an equivocation between the narrow and the broad readings.

I do not believe, however, that Thomson's argument actually does rely on such an equivocation. Presumably it is the narrow reading that is intended throughout the argument, and thus the transition from (ii) to (iii) is still in need of explanation. I suspect that Thomson would justify the transition through the use of an assumption that, unfortunately, she has not explicitly stated. Before we can supply this premise for her, however, some further discussion of (i) is necessary.

Even if we restrict our attention to nonevaluative facts, it is not clear that (i) is correct. Suppose that B did not cause A's injury, but C did. Is it the case, as Thomson puts it, that "there is nothing true of B which rules out that A's injury had the history described in (1)"? Admittedly, the fact that B did not cause A's injury is compatible with A's injury being of type (1). By way of contrast, it can be noted that the fact that C did cause the injury is not compatible with a history of type (1). But isn't it true of B that he lives in a world where C caused the injury? And this fact about B is clearly incompatible with the situation being of type

(1). Thus, it might be argued, it simply isn't true that so long as B did not causally contribute to the injury, everything about B is compatible with its being the case that the situation is of type (1).

This objection could be met by denying that the fact that B lives in a world where C caused the injury is a fact *about* B—that is, denying that this is something true *of* B. There may well be something to this metaphysical reply, but I do not think we need to discuss it here. For even if facts of this sort *can* legitimately be called facts about B, I doubt that Thomson meant to be claiming anything about such facts at all. She clearly had in mind a somewhat more limited set of facts when she claimed that nothing true of B ruled out the situation's being of type (1). At worst, then, we need to stipulatively restrict the scope of the expressions "facts about," "true of," and so on, yet again, so that they will exclude facts of the problematic kind. But how exactly is this to be done?

It won't do to understand the argument as referring only to intrinsic facts about B—ruling out relational facts. For it is clear that the scope of the expression "facts about B," and so on, is intended to include some relational facts as well. It is true that the fact that B lives in a world where C caused the injury is merely a relational fact about B, and we want to disregard this fact. But suppose it had been B that caused A's injury. This too would be a relational fact about B, and yet we would *not* want to disregard facts of this sort: it seems to be the right kind for inclusion as a fact *about* B. Thus the proposed restriction is too severe.

Rather than suggesting an alternative account of the desired restriction (something which, at any rate, I am unable to provide), I propose merely to label it. Facts about the fellow inhabitants of the world in which B lives seem too remote and external to be counted as facts *about* B in the relevant sense. On the other hand, facts about B's previous acts, or his motives (or his race, favorite foods, and so on) do seem sufficiently internal to count. Let us therefore call these *external* and *internal* facts, respectively.[5]

Once we understand the argument as referring to internal facts, (i) is more plausible. It is still not a trivial claim, of course: it relies on what we might grandiosely call a metaphysical judgment about the compatibility of states of affairs. But this judgment seems a plausible one to grant Thomson: if B did not causally contribute to A's injury then the internal

5. As should be clear, I am now using "internal/external" in a different sense than that of Section II. My use also differs from Thomson's use of these terms on pp. 128–32.

facts about B do seem to be compatible with that injury having a history of type (1). And so, given (i), we can conclude with (ii) that the internal facts about B are compatible with its being the case that B is not liable. But it is still not obvious how this enables us to move to the categorical assertion in (iii) that B is *not* liable.

I think we can make progress by considering the position of one who denies (iii). He holds that it is compatible with what we have been told about B, that B is liable. (B may not actually *be* liable, but nothing in the argument rules it out.) Thus one who denies (iii) but still accepts (ii) holds that all of the internal facts about B are compatible both with situations in which B is liable, and with situations in which B is not liable. But what would explain this difference in B's liability from the one kind of situation to the other? Obviously not a difference in the internal facts about B, for these stay the same: we are considering alternative situations compatible with the actual internal facts concerning B. Thus the difference in B's liability would have to arise from a difference in some of the *external* facts.

But Thomson may think such a position unreasonable. I suspect that Thomson believes that B's liability or nonliability must be determined solely by the *internal* facts about B. External facts have too little to do with B himself for it to be reasonable for them to play a role in determining B's liability. Thus the missing premise from Thomson's argument is

*Internalism*: A person's liability depends only upon internal facts about that person.

If internalism is true, and (ii) is correct, then (iii) must follow: if the internal facts about B are compatible with B's being nonliable, then—obviously enough—those facts are not themselves sufficient to ground B's liability; but since liability is based only upon internal facts, B must not, in fact, be liable.

Ultimately, then, Thomson's argument has three basic premises, and its structure seems to be the following: If B did not causally contribute to A's injury, then (given the metaphysical judgment) the internal facts about B are compatible with the injury being of type (1). This means (given the general judgment about cases of that type) that the internal facts about B are compatible with B's nonliability. Thus (given internalism) B cannot be liable. Therefore, causality is necessary for liability.

Before endorsing Thomson's argument, of course, we need to reexamine the basic premises, and see whether they should be accepted. But a preliminary observation may be in order. If her argument is sound, Thomson has succeeded in proving that causality matters for liability—and this is certainly a significant improvement over the mere appeal to intuition. But has she also met her goal of explaining *why* causality matters? This is less clear. We have the outline of an explanation, to be sure: causality is necessary for liability, because if someone has not causally contributed to harm, the internal facts about him are not sufficient to ground liability, for they cannot rule out a scenario in which he is nonliable. This is rather thin as an explanation, however, unless we also have an account of why liability must be grounded solely in the internal facts, and why others are not liable in cases of type (1). Thus we have all the more reason to examine the basic premises of Thomson's argument.

## IV

It is interesting to note that in my reconstruction of Thomson's argument, the notion of freedom of action has so far played no role—despite Thomson's assertions that it provides the key to understanding why causality matters for liability. Where it does enter the argument, according to Thomson, is as an explanation for the general judgment about cases of type (1). So let us begin with this judgment.

Recall the details of Thomson's general characterization of the cases in question:

(1) A caused A's injury, freely, wittingly, for purposes of his own; and no one other than A caused it, or even causally contributed to it (p. 110).

Thomson's claim is that, even if A later wants to undo the damage, given that we have a case of type (1)

B's freedom of action protects him against A: A is not entitled to call on B's assets for the purpose—A is not entitled to disrupt B's planning to reverse an outcome wholly of his own planning which he now finds unsatisfactory (p. 110).

Intuitively, we may well agree with Thomson that A is not entitled to seek "compensation" from B. But how does an appeal to B's freedom of action do anything to explain this? As always, if B were liable, this would be a restriction on his freedom of action, and thus could be justified only for a sufficient reason. Obviously enough, Thomson thinks that such a restriction is *not* justified. But what is the explanation for this judgment?

One might think that if the argument discussed in Section I had been successful it would have provided the necessary explanation. For if A is not entitled to seek compensation from a random individual, then—it seems—he is not entitled to seek it from B in the case at hand. But this is a mistake. For the conclusion of that argument was merely that someone could be liable only if he had some (yet to be identified) particular feature. For all that that argument showed, greater wealth, or having acted negligently, and so on, might be among the requisite features. And nothing in the case at hand rules out the possibility that B has one or another of these potentially relevant features. Since Thomson is after the general judgment that B is not liable, no matter *what* features B has— provided that we have a case of type (1)—nothing in the earlier argument will be of any use to her.

Presumably, then, Thomson thinks that there is something in particular about cases of type (1) that rules out B's liability. If we could identify the relevant feature of these cases, then no doubt we could say that—given that feature—making B liable would unjustifiably restrict his freedom of action. But Thomson's appeal to freedom of action does nothing to help us see what the relevant feature is; and it thus does nothing to explain the general judgment about cases of type (1).

One might try to provide Thomson with the missing account—isolating the relevant features of cases of type (1), and justifying the claim that those features rule out B's liability. But I will not attempt to offer such an account here. For it is puzzling why Thomson felt the need to bring in anything as complicated as cases of type (1) in the first place. Consider a much simpler type of case:

(O) A is not injured at all.

It seems obvious that B cannot be liable in cases of this type, for A is not in need of compensation at all. As we shall see, even this general judgment can be challenged, but surely anyone who accepts the judgment about cases of type (1) will accept the general judgment about cases of type (O). If this is so, Thomson could have argued as follows: even if A has in fact been injured, provided that B did not causally contribute to the injury, all of the *internal* facts about B are compatible with the situation being of type (O) in which B is not liable. Thus (given internalism) B is, in fact, not liable.

If Thomson's original argument is sound then, so far as I can see, this second version must be sound as well. Note that although the argument still relies on a general judgment about cases of a certain type, as well a a metaphysical judgment about compatibility, these two premises here seem to verge on the trivial. This suggests that the real work of the argument is being done by the assumption of internalism. Let us, therefore, turn to this central premise.

V

Internalism is the view that a person's liability must depend solely on internal facts about that person. Since Thomson did not even state this basic premise of her argument, we can only conjecture as to what her reasons would be for accepting it. Perhaps Thomson finds internalism intuitively evident, and this helps to explain why she did not recognize the need to state and defend it. For it is, I think, an intuitively attractive view. Indeed, many will want to give internalism a far broader scope than I have given it.

I have merely ascribed to Thomson the view that *liability* must depend on internal facts. But some, I think, would hold that the same is true for all moral requirements altogether. And others might hold that the basic *rights* that a person has must also depend solely upon internal facts about that person. Such internalistic theses, I believe, can go a long way toward explaining many common intuitions about morality; and they deserve careful examination. But here we can limit ourselves to the question of what justification there might be for accepting internalism with regard to liability.

As I have noted, such internalism seems to find support in the intuition that a person's liability must be grounded in facts sufficiently connected to the person himself. After all, we might wonder, how can an obligation for a given individual to pay compensation get a "grip" on that person, unless the relevant facts about the person himself allow it to get a "hold"? This is, for many, a powerful intuition. But until we are told how to cash out the metaphors, the intuition seems too vague to be by itself an adequate defense of internalism.

Interestingly enough, freedom of action again appears to offer the key to a possible account. If B's liability could turn on facts beyond his control, then his "moral space" would be in constant danger of shrinking or disappearing. Thus, it might be thought, freedom of action supports grounding liability only in facts over which the given individual has had the opportunity to exercise some control.

As it happens, not even all *internal* facts about B will satisfy this test (consider, for example, race). But this will not hurt Thomson's argument. Internalism merely claims that liability is determined solely on the basis of internal facts. Freedom of action may support an even bolder assertion—that liability is determined solely on the basis of internal facts over which B has had some control. But if the bolder assertion is true, then internalism is true as well. And that is all that Thomson needs for her argument.

Unfortunately, freedom of action does not actually support internalism at all. For internalism claims that liability is determined *solely* on the basis of internal facts. At best, freedom of action supports the conclusion that among the conditions necessary for grounding liability, *some* must be under the given individual's control. Provided that this is so, however, there is no reason why there should not be *additional* conditions necessary for liability, and among these might be the obtaining of external facts over which the individual has no control.

The same problem arises, I think, even for the vague intuition that there must be some fact about the individual by virtue of which an obligation to pay compensation is able to get a "hold." At best, this intuition supports the view that internal facts must be among the necessary conditions for grounding liability. It does not support the claim of internalism that liability must depend on the internal facts alone.

Could Thomson's argument work if she retreated to the more modest claim that internal facts must be among the necessary grounds for liability? I do not think so. Thomson's argument turns on the claim that if B did not causally contribute to the injury, then the internal facts about B are compatible with a scenario in which B is not liable. But by itself, this only shows that the internal facts coupled with one possible set of external facts yield nonliability. Unless we think that the internal facts are the only ones relevant for liability, we will have no reason to rule out the possibility that the internal facts yield B's liability when coupled with the external facts that actually obtain.

Thus Thomson does need internalism for her argument to succeed, yet I can see no obvious way to defend it. This does not, of course, prove that internalism is false. But it does leave a significant gap in Thomson's argument.

If it *could* be shown that internalism is false, that would deal a fatal blow to the argument. However, I do not think that such a demonstration can be easily provided. Internalism, to be sure, faces serious problems. But it is far from clear to what extent it can meet them.

For example, it seems plausible to hold that B's liability may turn in part on whether or not A gave his permission to be injured. The existence of A's permission, however, does not appear to be an internal fact about B. Thus we seeem to be provided with a straightforward counterexample to internalism. This conclusion is too hasty, however, for there are at least two ways in which an internalist might try to meet the objection (other than rejecting the relevance of A's permission). First, it might be claimed that although the existence of A's permission is an external fact, there is an *internal* fact about B that corresponds to it: the fact that B acted with A's permission. If this is indeed a legitimate internal fact, attention to it should enable the internalist to sort out the various cases appropriately. (Or perhaps one could make do with the internal fact about B that he took himself to be acting with A's permission.) Second, one might modify internalism. Rather than claiming that B's liability must depend solely upon internal facts about B, one might hold that B's liability to A must depend solely upon internal facts about the *relation* that holds between B and A. Since A's having permitted B's act would be an internal fact about the relation between the two, such a modified internalist could recognize the relevance of this fact to B's liability.

I do not know whether either of these possibilities could be adequately defended. (Nor is it clear whether the second alternative would be compatible with Thomson's argument.) Examining these responses, however—not to mention considering other possible objections and replies— would obviously require a fuller account of internalism than we have room to develop here. As a consequence, I am simply going to avoid taking a position on whether or not internalism is true.

However, even if we leave the issue of the truth of internalism unresolved, the fact remains that Thomson's argument appeals to internalism without defending it. Yet in the absence of such a defense, it seems plausible to think that Thomson's argument merely begs the question. That is, I believe that Thomson's use of internalism begs the question against one who denies that causality is necessary for liability.

The denial that causality is necessary for liability is, of course, compatible with a variety of alternative views about what liability actually requires. It is not possible to survey more than a few such alternative views here; but these should, I think, suffice to show that Thomson's unsupported appeal to internalism is illegitimate.

Consider, first, the view of one who holds that when A has been injured against his will (perhaps by C, who has since died), A is entitled to seek compensation from B by virtue of B's greater wealth. Such a person might well hold that were A *uninjured* he would have no claim on B's funds, but since he *has* in fact been injured, he is entitled to seek the cost of damages from the wealthier B. On this view, B's liability depends, in part, on whether or not A has been injured by some third party. But this fact about A's injury is surely not an internal fact about B. Thus, on this view, B's liability partly turns on an external fact; that is, the view involves the rejection of internalism. Therefore, obviously enough, it would simply be begging the question to attempt to refute this view by assuming internalism without defending it.

As a second possibility, consider the view of one who holds that if A has been injured against his will (perhaps by C, who has since died), he is entitled to seek compensation from B by virtue of B's having negligently performed an act that ran a great risk of injuring A. (Perhaps B and C performed similar risky acts, but through mere chance C's act caused an injury, while B's act did not.) Such a person might well hold that had A not been injured he would not be entitled to seek funds from B, but since he was injured, he is entitled to seek the cost of damages from the negligent B. On this second view, as with the first, B's liability turns in part on an external fact about A's injury. Thus this view, too, involves the rejection of internalism, and Thomson's failure to defend internalism means that her argument begs the question against it.

Both of these views agree with Thomson that A's being entitled to seek compensation depends in part on his having been injured. Since they deny that causality is necessary for liability, however, the dispute between Thomson and these views partly comes down to the question of whether the external fact of A's having been injured by someone else can be relevant to B's liability. Internalism, of course, would simply rule this possibility out a priori. But that is the very reason why an undefended assumption of internalism in an argument against these views is illegitimate.

It may be instructive to consider, as a final possibility, the view of one who holds that when B has negligently performed a risky act toward A, A is entitled to seek funds from B—whether or not A has actually been injured by B or by anyone else. It may be somewhat strained (or perhaps even inappropriate) to speak of "compensation" here, for there is no injury that is being corrected. But one who holds this view may well believe that even if B's act *had* injured A, this would affect only the appropriateness of the label "compensation," and not the grounds of B's liability: the latter would still be grounded simply in the fact that B had negligently performed the risky act.

Notice that this view, unlike the others, does not involve the rejection of internalism. Thus in this case, at least, Thomson's undefended assumption of internalism does not beg the question. But, unfortunately, her argument fails here for a different reason. For one who holds this view will deny the general judgment about cases of type (1). Admittedly, in such cases, A's injury is irrelevant for the question of whether A is entitled to seek funds from B. But in some cases of type (1), B will have negligently performed a risky act, and this will be sufficient to ground B's liability. So it is false—according to the view under discussion—that in cases of type (1) B is never liable. For similar reasons, the general judgment about cases of type (O) will be rejected as well. Without these general judgments, of course, Thomson's argument cannot proceed. But to assume these judgments, without more adequate defense than has been provided, begs the question yet again.

It is also worth noting that someone who holds the view we are discussing might, in fact, attempt to defend it through an appeal to internalism. He might argue that the question of whether or not a risky act *actually* results in injury—depending as it does on mere chance—is insufficiently connected to B himself to count as an internal fact. Thus, he might insist, an adequate account of internalism would rule out the possibility that causality can matter for liability. In short, the very assumption of internalism, on which Thomson's argument turns, might be thought to support the rejection of Thomson's own conclusion. There is no room to pursue this dispute here, but it should serve to underscore the significance of Thomson's failure to provide an explicit account and defense of internalism.

It is not my intention to discuss whether any of the three views I have just sketched are particularly plausible; for our purposes here that should not matter. Thomson has attempted to argue that causality is necessary for liability. I have claimed that her argument relies on premises that would be straightforwardly rejected by many who deny her conclusion. In the absence of an adequate defense of these premises, it seems to me that Thomson's argument simply begs the question.

This is not to say that Thomson's argument is unsound. For all that I have shown to the contrary, it might well be that Thomson's premises are correct. But three negative conclusions still seem to be in order. First, I take it that Thomson was trying to offer a *demonstration* that causality is necessary for liability. That is, she was trying to offer an argument that would satisfy even those not already convinced of her conclusions. Given the lack of defense of a controversial premise, this attempt, I think, must be judged inadequate. Second, Thomson set out to explain *why* causality matters for liability. She claimed that the key to the desired explanation could be found in the importance of freedom of action. If my criticisms have been correct, however, the appeal to freedom of action has been little more than a placeholder for the appeal to intuition. So far as I can see, Thomson has not shown that freedom of action would play any significant role in an explanation of why causality matters for liability.[6] Finally, I have suggested that the explanation Thomson does offer actually relies most centrally on the assumption of internalism. But internalism is obscure as well as controversial. Without an adequate account of it, it seems to me that we have no real explanation of why causality matters for liability.

6. Noting that it is implausible to hold that causality is *sufficient* for liability (p. 111), Thomson suggests that "considerations of freedom of action will take us a long way—not merely into the question why causality matters, but also into the question when and where it does" (p. 116). Her argument (p. 115) is baffling, however. She suggests, plausibly, that given A's freedom of action, if B knows he will injure A, he must buy the right to do so in advance, if he can. She concludes, again plausibly, that if B knows he will injure A, but due to A's absence cannot buy the right to do so in advance, he must—nonetheless—pay for the right afterward, by compensating A. If this is so, however, as far as I can see A's freedom of action should equally support the following conclusion: even if B does not know he will injure A (because B will injure A by a freak accident that B could not reasonably have been expected to foresee), and so B justifiably fails to buy the right to injure A in advance, he must—nonetheless—pay for the right afterward, by compensating A. Yet Thomson denies that B is liable in cases of this latter sort, and she mysteriously implies without explanation that freedom of action justifies her judgment.

JUDITH JARVIS THOMSON     A Note on Internalism

We have the intuition that causation is necessary for liability: that the one or ones who caused the harm are the one or ones who must pay for it. The intuition is strong, but overrideable. Other considerations are also important to us in deciding whom to impose liability on, and more broadly in deciding what liability-imposing legal system we should adopt; and we may decide that on balance it is better (because on balance fairer, or for some other reason) that liability be imposed on some who cannot be shown to have caused a harm, or even on some who are known not to have caused it. On balance—for we feel the burden of proof to lie on the other considerations.

I wished to get at, not why we think it unfair or wrong to impose liability in the absence of causality, for that is not true, but rather why we feel that absence of causality *needs* overriding.[1]

Shelly Kagan argues that in tracing our route to that intuition I assume the truth of a doctrine he calls "internalism," which says that "a person's liability depends only upon internal facts about that person."[2] He objects that I give no argument for that doctrine. He is right: I do assume something like that doctrine, and I do not argue for it. I think it a valuable contribution on his part to have drawn attention to that doctrine, for I think that it and some of its cousins are of interest to moral theory. I cannot do more at this time than make a few comments about it and them, because it is not even clear to me what is the most plausible way of expressing the ideas at work here.

1. I regret that my article did not make clear to Fischer and Ennis how limited my intention was—though I confess to surprise that it did not, given the conclusions it came to about *Summers v. Tice* and *Sindell.*

2. Shelly Kagan, "Causation and Liability," *Philosophy & Public Affairs* 15, no. 1 (this issue): 41.

I ought to begin with an account of what marks internal facts about a person off from external facts about him. As Kagan says, any friend of internalism would count the fact that B lives in a world in which C shot A in the leg as an external fact about B; by contrast, the fact that B shot A in the leg is an internal fact about B. But I cannot produce such an account, and must leave the difference to intuition.[3]

So let us turn to internalism. I think it helps to see what internalism involves if we contrast liability with the concept 'what a person ought to do.' It is certainly plausible to think that the question what a person ought to do does not everywhere turn just on internal facts about him. Suppose B is rich. (That is an internal fact about B.) Suppose A acquires a need which he cannot meet himself. (The fact that B lives in a world in which that is true is an external fact about B.) Perhaps there are people who would say that the conjunction of these two facts by itself yields that B ought to give A money. Most of us, I fancy, would want to hear a good bit more about A and his need before agreeing that B ought to give A money. (Is A nearby? Is his need urgent and sudden? Is C already on the way with help? And so on.) Nevertheless it does seem plausible to think that the fact that B is rich does not by itself yield that B ought to give A money (after all, the fact that B is rich is compatible with A's being even richer), *and* that there might well be a set of facts about A and his need which, in conjunction with the fact that B is rich, does yield that B ought to give A money.

Now the question whether B is liable for compensation to A for an injury suffered by A is not the same as the question whether B ought to pay such and such an amount to A, where the such and such amount would compensate A for the injury.[4] The liability ascription is in one way weaker, for it is consistent to suppose that B is liable and that it is all the same not the case that B ought to pay. The liability ascription is in another

3. Here moral theory makes contact with metaphysics—for I should think that producing such an account would require attending to the difference between real change and what Peter Geach called 'Cambridge' change. (See Peter Geach, *God and the Soul* [New York: Schocken Books, 1969], pp. 71–72.) If a thing acquires a property which it formerly lacked, then it undergoes a Cambridge change: thus if Socrates acquires the property 'is shorter than Theaetetus' which Socrates formerly lacked, then Socrates has undergone a Cambridge change. But he may not have also undergone a real change. He did undergo a real change if he acquired that property because he shrank; he did not undergo a real change if he acquired that property because Theaetetus grew.

4. Certainly the question before the court in a tort suit is not whether the defendant ought to pay the plaintiff's bills. If that were the question, much would be relevant evidence that is not.

way, and more interestingly, stronger, for it ascribes a duty and a cor-relative claim-right. (I shall henceforth be using "duty" in Hohfeld's way, namely, strictly as correlative of "claim-right.") If B is liable for compensation to A for an injury suffered by A, then B is under a duty to compensate A, and A has a claim-right that B compensate him. Kagan sometimes talks as if the question whether B is liable for compensation to A were the same as the question whether "A is entitled to seek compensation from B." But that is *far* too weak. The question at issue is whether A is entitled to *be* compensated by B.

I am sorry that I did not make sufficiently clear (because I did not sufficiently clearly see) the relevance of this difference to the project I had in view.

As Kagan says, there are other internalistic theses. I suggest we reserve the name "internalism" for the class, and speak instead of internalism about liability—as opposed, for example, to internalism about this or that other kind of duty, or about duty generally, and more importantly, as opposed to internalism about what a person ought to do. As I have indicated, internalism about what a person ought to do seems to me very implausible. So an argument for internalism about liability would have to focus on the differences among duties (supposing that there are relevant differences among duties), and on the differences between duties on the one hand, and what a person ought to do on the other hand.

But the prior question really is what exactly internalism about liability should be taken to *say*. According to the version Kagan offers as my hidden premise, B is liable for compensation to A for an injury suffered by A if and only if internal facts about B by themselves make it true that he is. But that is far too strong. For B is not liable for compensation to A for an injury suffered by A unless A is in fact injured; so according to Kagan's version of internalism about liability, B is not liable unless internal facts about him entail that A was injured. If B caused A to be injured, then there is an internal fact about him which entails that A was injured. But liability *can* be acquired in other ways than by causing an injury. My rich uncle, for example, or my insurance agent, might commit himself to compensating my future victims for any injuries I may later cause them, in which case he will be under a duty to compensate them when they get injured, even if neither his making that commitment, nor any other internal facts about him entail that those people do get injured.

In light of the familiar possibility of acquiring liability by virtue of having made a commitment, it might well be asked why I said at the outset that we have the intuition that causation is necessary for liability. Well, our intuition is, rather, that commitments of appropriate kinds apart, causation is necessary for liability.

One way of construing internalism about liability, then, is to take it as similarly constrained, that is, as saying only that commitments of appropriate kinds apart, liability turns only on internal facts.

A second way of construing it is to make it incorporate commitment in some way. That a man said to me "I promise to compensate all your future victims" is itself an internal fact about him; and it is important about duties generally that they can be generated by that kind of internal fact too, that is, as well as by internal facts which consist in one's causing this or that.

There are two kinds of commitment which can generate duties. First are the unconditional commitments, such as I make if I say to you "I promise you I will never again eat a banana." If I say that to you, then I am under a duty to never again eat a banana—nothing else need be the case for me to be under that duty than my making the commitment. Second are the conditional commitments, such as I make if I say to you "I promise you that if you pay me five dollars, then I will never again eat a banana." If I say that to you, then I suppose it could be said I am under a conditional duty—to never again eat a banana if you pay me five dollars—but I am anyway not under a duty to never again eat a banana unless it turns out to be the case that you do pay me five dollars.

A man who says to me "I promise to compensate all your future victims" makes a conditional commitment; and he is not under a duty to compensate (as it might be) Jones, unless I injure Jones. An internalism about liability which attempts to incorporate commitment would have to allow for the role in generating the duty which is played by a fact external to the commitment maker where the commitment he made was conditional.

There are other ways of acquiring duties than by causing this or that and by committing oneself. The adoption of new political or legal arrangements may generate new duties in the members of this or that group. And it is arguable that even social arrangements apart there are other ways of acquiring duties. Thus on some views we have a duty to care for our parents if they are old and in need of care simply by virtue of the fact that we are their children—or perhaps instead (or also) in virtue of having received benefits from them. Presumably the duty to compensate for an injury can itself be acquired in some of these ways, and perhaps internalism about liability should incorporate them too.

So I do not even know how best to express internalism about liability, and *a fortiori* do not know how to argue for it.

What does seem clear, however, is that what a person ought to do is sensitive to external facts in ways in which duty is not. Suppose, for example, that A is in need of aid, and that B alone can provide it. Before we settle on whether or not B ought to provide the aid, we need to know (among other things) what it would cost B to provide it, and how grave a harm A will suffer if he is not provided with it. What is to be noticed, however, is that supposing a fixed level of cost to B, the answer to the question whether B ought to provide the aid will vary with the gravity of the harm which A will suffer if B does not provide it. Thus, for example, suppose it would be seriously inconvenient for B to provide the needed aid. Then perhaps he ought to provide it all the same if A will otherwise suffer a grave harm—for example, the loss of his legs. But as we imagine the harm which A will otherwise suffer to be less and less grave—down from (as it might be) loss of legs to loss of finger to loss of hat to loss of newspaper—we somewhere along the way conclude that it no longer is the case that B ought to provide the aid. Perhaps we have reached that point when we get down to loss of hat; anyway, I shall suppose so. That is, I am supposing that where it would be seriously inconvenient for B to provide the aid without which A will lose his hat, it is not the case that B ought to provide it. I stress: it is not as if B ought to provide the aid, while having a good excuse for not doing so, it just is not the case that he ought to. In short, given a fixed cost to B, what he ought to do is highly sensitive to facts about others.

Not so duties. Suppose that C is in need of aid, and that D alone can provide it—just as in the case of A and B. But suppose we make one or other of the following additions to the story of C and D: D himself caused C to be in need of the aid,[5] or D made a prior commitment to C to provide the aid if and when needed. Then (other things being equal) D is under

---

5. Some people who argue that we must provide aid to the needy in third-world countries appeal only to their need and our wealth, which supports the conclusion that we ought to provide the aid. Others appeal in addition to something quite different: they say "And moreover, our past economic practices are responsible for that need." I take them to be arguing for the stronger claim, namely, that we are under a duty of providing the aid.

a duty to provide it. Let us fix the cost to D of providing the aid at the same level as the cost to B of providing it, namely, serious inconvenience, and vary the harm which C will otherwise suffer—down from loss of legs to loss of finger to loss of hat to loss of newspaper. Duty itself affects what one ought to do, and I think we therefore have to go further down the progression before we get to a point at which we conclude that it no longer is the case that D ought to provide the aid. Perhaps we do not reach that point until we get down to loss of newspaper; anyway, I should think we have reached it there. But throughout the progression down it remains true that D is under a duty to provide the aid. This is shown by the fact that even when we get down to the point at which it is not true that D ought to provide the aid, that is, the point at which C will otherwise suffer only loss of newspaper, D cannot simply fail to provide the aid and then wash his hands of the matter—if D fails to provide the aid so that C loses his newspaper, then D must get him another. (By contrast, if B fails to provide the aid so that A loses his hat, B need not get him another.) Whether a person is under a duty to aid, then, is not in the same way sensitive to external facts about others.

Considerations of the kind I point to here are, of course, matters of intuition, but not merely matters of intuition: these are among the intuitions which show us what the concept of duty *is*.[6]

We may think of a person as living within certain moral spaces. One of them is fixed by what it is morally permissible for him to do—that is, by what it is not the case that he ought not do. He is entirely free to act as he wishes within that space in the sense that whatever he does within that space it is morally permissible that he do. A second of his moral spaces is fixed by what he is under no duty not to do—that is, by what no one has any claim-right against him that he not do. He is entirely free to act as he wishes within that space in the sense that whatever he does

6. Kagan's attitude toward intuition strikes me as very worrisome. He says that "without a plausible account [of the intuition that causation is necessary for liability] our confidence in this view is probably unwarranted; at the very least, our understanding of ethics will remain inadequate." I don't think he says this because he has reason to think the intuition is *false*—anyway, he gives no such reason. I think he thinks an unanchored intuition is suspect simply by virtue of being unanchored. But unless morality can be got from truths outside morality, it will perforce rest on *some* moral intuitions or other. Should we really conclude that our confidence in it or them is 'probably unwarranted'? And: what makes our present understanding of ethics inadequate is, not that it rests on intuition, but that it rests on scattered intuitions—what we lack is a way of seeing how the intuitions hang together to form a theory.

within that space is no infringement of any claim-right. (Hohfeld speaks here, not of freedom, but of privileges or liberties.) Then the first of the points which seems to come out of a consideration of the contrast between A and B on the one hand, and C and D on the other, could be re-expressed in terms of this metaphor: the first space grows and shrinks with different external facts in ways in which the second does not.

A second point is that the first space grows and shrinks when the second space does, for as I said, duty itself affects what one ought to do. In some cases the effect is direct: for example, I am the one who is under a duty to clean the blackboards this week, so I am the one who ought to do it, despite the fact that you could do it just as easily. In other cases the effect is indirect: there are cases in which the demands of morality are met if I do not do what I am under a duty to do, but instead make amends for the harm I cause by not doing it. (Unless a duty is absolute—that is, unless it is the correlative of an absolute claim-right—it is over-rideable. The duty to compensate is not absolute, and that is why the intuition we began with is overrideable.) It is important to us, then, just what are the limits of our freedom in the second sense, and that not merely because this is an intrinsically interesting question, but also because of their bearing on the limits of our freedom in the first sense.

I suspect now that it is because of the special impact which a person's acquiring a duty has on what he ought to do, and thus on the extent of his freedom in the first sense, that duties are acquired only in the narrow range of ways which would be characterized by a plausible version of internalism about duty, if such a thing could be got. But these are mere comments in passing. The varieties of internalism call for closer attention than I can give them now.

THOMAS W. POGGE     Liberalism and
Global Justice:
Hoffmann and Nardin
on Morality in
International Affairs

Most of Stanley Hoffmann's published work is devoted to topics in comparative and international politics and U.S. foreign policy. The lectures collected in his *Duties Beyond Borders* focus on some central problems in international ethics, each considered in connection with current issues and choices in foreign policy. The topics of philosophical interest addressed here include the theory of the just war and its application to questions about the justifiability of nuclear deterrence; the meaning and moral importance of international order; human rights and how foreign policy can and cannot effectively promote respect for them; and international distributive justice. The discussions of these topics are not held together by any very clear general theory, but they do exhibit a common approach. Characteristic of this approach is a liberal concern for the individual as the ultimate subject of political theory and a recognition of an overriding imperative of realism. Taken together, these yield a commitment to moderation that is central to each of Hoffmann's discussions.

Terry Nardin's study of the genesis and character of international law and morality touches on many of the same philosophical issues as Hoffmann's, but does not for the most part take up their application to foreign policy. It does, however, fill in much historical detail about the development of international relations and institutions and the evolution of international law. Also in contrast to Hoffmann's book, Nardin's sets forth a general thesis about international morality. It holds that the norms of international morality must be uncommitted to, and thus neutral between, alternative conceptions of the individual and social good. I shall

The following books are discussed in this review essay: Stanley Hoffmann, *Duties Beyond Borders* (Syracuse: Syracuse University Press, 1981); Terry Nardin, *Law, Morality, and the Relations of States* (Princeton: Princeton University Press, 1983).

focus here on the moral and philosophical side of this thesis at the expense of the support Nardin wishes to draw from the history of international legal theory and doctrine.

While discussing these two books, this review essay also seeks to clarify and defend a recently developing approach to morality in foreign affairs that is characterized by two elements: it is liberal in orientation and it focuses on the assessment of *institutions* (rather than on that of conduct and policies within some existing global regime).[1] I hope that, properly explained, this approach might become attractive to many of its current critics who are similarly distressed, after all, by current levels of violence and deprivation. The two works to be reviewed are critical of this approach, each challenging one element of the position to be defended. Hoffmann attacks the emphasis on institutions, while Nardin comes into conflict with the moral commitments of liberalism. Before discussing their work, however, let me briefly introduce these two elements.

One main reason for laying stress on the institutional structure is that while liberal values make demands both on institutions and on the conduct of actors (citizens, officials, associations, and governments), the latter is in turn very largely determined, at least probabilistically, by the institutional scheme of penalties and incentives (the "payoff-matrix") which those actors confront. Thus, for example, the extent to which basic rights are actually enjoyed in some society will depend on its legal system, on the organization of its police forces, and so on. Similarly, the distribution pattern of income and wealth, and thus the incidence of dependence and poverty, will depend on economic arrangements such as the system of land tenure and the tax structure. The emphasis on institutions is then supported by the statistical fact that different institutional arrangements engender very different (and rather stable) levels of crime, apathy, political and economic inequality, and so forth.[2]

1. Notable examples are Part III of Charles Beitz, *Political Theory and International Relations* (Princeton: Princeton University Press, 1979) and D.A.J. Richards, "International Distributive Justice," *Ethics, Economics, and the Law*, ed. J. R. Pennock and J. W. Chapman (New York: New York University Press, 1982). See also T. W. Pogge, "Globalizing Justice as Fairness," unpublished manuscript. This new approach was largely inspired, it seems, by the work of John Rawls who shows, for the domestic case, how our liberal convictions can ground a moral critique of the major institutions (or the "basic structure") of a self-sufficient social system. I shall therefore call this approach Rawlsian, without however meaning to suggest that Rawls himself subscribes to its international application.

2. There are startling differences of this kind even among (roughly equally developed) Western societies such as Japan, the U.S., and Sweden. East/West contrasts tend to be even more pronounced.

Although comparative statistics are problematic on the global plane, the analogous point would seem to hold: Particular economic arrangements (say an international laissez-faire market with minimal constraints on distribution) will lead to some rather stable degree of inequality with concomitant rates of poverty, illiteracy, malnutrition, disease, and starvation. Similarly, political arrangements (say military competition in the absence of effective institutions for the creation, application, and enforcement of international law) will generate quite predictable overall levels of violence—within and between nations.[3]

If this picture is at least roughly correct empirically, then one rationale for focusing on institutions is the hope that in this way our combined moral efforts may accumulate into lasting progress. Concentrating on the mitigation of grievances, one could at best hope to maintain the world somewhat above its equilibrium point (where it would be if all people rationally pursued their own interests). Institutional change, on the other hand, might move that equilibrium point itself, thereby preparing the ground for further institutional change. Moral conduct is likely to be of enduring historical significance only if it can become cumulative in this way. Of course we may still end up concluding that there is no realistic and morally viable avenue of institutional change that would lead to a juster global regime. But such a pessimistic conclusion would presuppose a thorough analysis of institutional options with their coordinate paths of transition.

The other, *liberal* element of global liberalism is more familiar and can be stated briefly. The main idea is that a conception of social justice must take persons as the ultimate units of moral concern.[4] This concern is not

3. The considerations advanced in the last two paragraphs do not prejudge the issue of personal responsibility in any way. Thus, explaining a high crime rate by reference to institutional factors need not at all exonerate the (political or ordinary) criminals. It *may* exonerate them if their situation left them no feasible and morally preferable alternative option. In the latter vein Rawls argues that an unjust economic system may lead to unacceptable poverty through no fault of any participants, who cannot possibly conduct their transactions so as to preserve an acceptable distribution of assets. See John Rawls, "The Basic Structure as Subject," *Values and Morals*, ed. A. I. Goldman and J. Kim (Dortrecht: Reidel, 1978), section IV.

4. Rawls gives a fairly representative statement of this tenet on pp. 264f. of *A Theory of Justice* (Cambridge, MA: Harvard University Press, 1971). The same idea receives at least nominal endorsement even from Michael Walzer, perhaps the most vocal liberal advocate of "state rights" when he says that the "rights of political communities . . . belong to states, but they derive ultimately from the rights of individuals, and from them they take their force," *Just and Unjust Wars* (New York: Basic Books, 1977), p. 53. A counterinstance is Brian Barry who holds that states have rights vis-à-vis one another that are independent

tied to any particular conception of the good life, but rather seeks to protect the autonomy of individuals: their ability to develop their own interests and ambitions, to shape their own lives, and to participate in collective activities and endeavors. A liberal will then assess institutions (such as, on the global plane, alternative arrangements of the world economy or alternative circumscriptions of national sovereignty) by the extent to which they engender and support personal autonomy. Institutional schemes are judged by how well they provide for or protect certain fundamental civil liberties, elementary subsistence needs, and rights to participation in political decision making and to minimal education and health care.[5]

## I

The discussion of Hoffmann's work will focus on three controversial issues. My conclusion will be that the differences Hoffmann sees between himself and the new global liberals are more apparent than real, that his recommendations can be accommodated almost entirely within the framework he attacks.

The first issue is interpretive: Even in discussing the Rawlsian approach explicitly, Hoffmann is not altogether clear about the position he is rejecting. In particular, he largely misses the emphasis on institutions. Thus he charges that devising principles of justice

> is practically meaningless in the international milieu, because . . . in a milieu where self-help is the rule and where force can always be used by each agent, there is no guarantee whatsoever that these principles would ever stick for very long. (p. 4)

But this realization—that in the existing scheme compliance with moral rules is problematic—is precisely what motivates the attempt to construct principles of justice that would give rise to an international order where self-help is not the rule and where force can not always be used.

---

of and not reducible to individual rights. (See Barry, "Humanity and Justice in Global Perspective," in *Ethics, Economics, and the Law*, p. 248.)

5. There is of course some room for disagreement about the appropriate notion of personal autonomy and the optimal package of basic rights. The general contours I shall sketch in what follows will therefore be characteristic of a whole family of potential liberal conceptions of global justice. I cannot here provide a more detailed explication and defense of this approach, but see the works cited in footnote 3.

An analogous misunderstanding affects Hoffmann's discussion of Rawls's difference principle which (he asserts), when interpreted globally, would entail "a duty to minimize intrastate inequality . . . so as to maximize the position of the globally least advantaged group" (p. 154). But the difference principle applies not to actors but to institutions. Its point is not to exhort actors to redistribute part of their share in some prior distribution so as to achieve a more egalitarian pattern of holdings. Rather, the aim is to reform that scheme of institutions which determines how things get distributed in the first place. (Here the optimal scheme may of course involve "redistributive" *mechanisms* such as a progressive income tax.)[6]

Thus, it misses the point to complain that global liberalism is utopian because it imposes impossible burdens on the well off:

> Before I can spend a penny on the poor in the Appalachians, I have to spend all I can on those who are infinitely poorer in Bangladesh. This is not the way politics can work. (p. 4)

It is precisely *because* it would be unrealistic to expect widespread destitution to be staved off in perpetuity through voluntary contributions that advocates of something like a globalized difference principle seek a gradual reorganization of the world economy to the point where such deprivations are minimized.[7]

The second issue, the substantive analogue of the first, has to do with the perspective of analysis, with what is to be chosen as the (as it were) independent variable. Here Hoffmann's principal focus is on the important "players" within the U.S.—he discusses briefly the possible contributions by intellectuals, educators, and the media, but concentrates most of his attention on the U.S. government. The book thus assumes the perspective of politicians, asking what policies they should adopt so as to give other politicians greater incentives to respect and promote liberal values. As Hoffmann shows for topic after topic, our politicians can and

6. The quotation displays confusion also about the *content* of the difference principle which does not demand that inequality be minimized, but rather *requires* inequality insofar as that benefits everyone. Institutional options allowing social and economic inequality are then compared by assessing how much each would benefit those whom it benefits least. (Not in all contexts, but only in this single respect of institutionally engendered inequality does the difference principle call for maximizing the position of the least advantaged.)

7. Even at home we must, it seems, rely on *institutional* mechanisms—or where does Hoffmann see significant tangible concern for the poor in Appalachia?

do act more or less well morally. Still, their option space is subject to two weighty constraints: They must (1) heed public opinion at home to avoid "a domestic backlash"; they "cannot go so far ahead as to be rejected" (pp. 23, 157). And even the most well-intentioned statesman must (2) act rationally toward the other players on the "geopolitical map of enmities and alignments" (p. 125)—above all, one's conduct must not be exploitable by the "other side."

On this analysis it would then be a crucial task of moral politics to work toward relaxing these two constraints so as to make them more encouraging of moral conduct. Here one might well end up concluding that the main moral failing of those in positions of authority is their lack of support for, or outright resistance to, (1) the formation of a more cosmopolitan public consciousness[8] and (2) institutional reform toward global conditions more supportive of individual rights.

It is the second type of improvement especially that globalist Rawlsians would aim at. They should conceive of the global institutional scheme as their independent variable, which is to be adjusted so that, assuming rational policies on the part of the main players, violence and deprivation will become ever less likely. In taking this perspective, one is rejecting a main strand of Hoffmann's position: the hope that "exhortations" (p. 204) for restraint and moderation on our side may lead to a gradual escalation of good behavior among the main players and thus to a "morally acceptable international milieu" (p. 1). First of all, it is not clear how the minor (or non-)players, the destitute and oppressed, would gain if the more powerful governments learned to get along. And, more to the point, the idea that somehow the atmosphere could improve in the absence of institutional change seems, in light of the past forty years, to show the very lack of realism with which Hoffmann likes to reproach his utopian opponents. No détente will last so long as the domestic and global clout of the crucial players, stronger militarily than economically, is significantly enhanced by a climate of international hostility.

These considerations undermine only one strand of Hoffmann's view—leaving intact his (similarly unrealistic) exhortations to be nice to the

---

8. Here Hoffmann speaks of nurturing the fragile "germs of cosmopolitanism" (p. 39):

the scope of our obligation to individuals in other societies varies in time and in space. There was none of it perhaps sixty or fifty years ago (or rather, very few people acknowledged one). There is some now, more widely recognized. If all goes well, and statesmen, writers, and so on, press on, it may grow in the future (p. 157).

Have statesmen really been pressing?

little players, and his own program for institutional change. In the latter category, he advocates "a large measure of institutionalization in international affairs" (p. 205)—specifically, "an international non-proliferation regime" (p. 218), a "*jus ante et contra bellum*" (p. 82), "a reinforcement of regional and international institutions" (p. 213), and various economic mechanisms to reduce global inequality (pp. 177–81). It is proposals of just this kind that a Rawlsian conception of global justice would seek to argue for and specify. And so the second disagreement boils down in the end to little more than a different allocation of emphasis between psychological and institutional factors.

The third issue, finally, is that Hoffmann—as historian and political scientist rather than moral philosopher (cf. p. 1)—is "starting from what is and groping toward the 'ought' " (p. 2). Rather than specify an ideal institutional scheme as a long-term objective that might guide present liberal strategy, he wants to start from a thorough understanding of the status quo: of the directions in which change is possible and of the presently existing forces that might bring it about. It is not clear from the text what significance Hoffmann attaches to this contrast. There are at least two possibilities. One might envision merely a division of labor, something Hoffmann perhaps has in mind when he says that "uplifted politics and applied ethics ought to converge" (p. 2): The moral philosopher must not insist on an ideal that is not connectible to the status quo by any feasible path of transition; and the political scientist should base his choice of short- or medium-term goals in part upon what contributions these would make to the realization of morally favored ideals.

But the contrast might also involve a more substantive claim, namely that a (partly) moralized political science is of much greater importance than philosophical ideal theory. Showing this would require Hoffmann to defend a strong version of at least one of the following two propositions:

(a) The general direction in which things should move is rather obvious, and in assessing feasible changes one can thus safely do without ideal theory.

(b) The philosophers' ideals are historically quite out of reach, even in the long run, and debating their merits is therefore largely a waste of time.

Concerning (a), Hoffmann would agree, I believe, that progress requires more than getting right some very complicated technical questions about means (though the choice of effective means is what most of his book is about). Even obviously desirable objectives—provisions for human rights and subsistence needs, détente, non-proliferation, and curbing arms sales—are not beyond the need of a reasoned defense against influential interests often inclined to put honorable philosophical concepts (that of freedom most frequently) to rather surprising uses. And those same objectives must also be balanced against one another so as to set priorities toward a coherent political strategy (cf. p. 116). In these respects the discussion of even quite distant ideals can play an important motivating and clarifying role, just as, I would think, Rawls's "learned and massive tome" (p. 2) has done in the debate about domestic justice.

Concerning (b), Hoffmann humorously demolishes some more outlandish proposals by utopian writers (e.g., that the number of states should be reduced to twenty-five—p. 192). Yet he does not reject the project to "move progressively toward Falk's idea of a new system or world order, not based on the nation-state" (pp. 139f.) as infeasible, and thus can hardly dismiss post-Rawlsian authors on this ground, especially if *one* criterion for their assessment of ideals is precisely the likelihood that these ideals can be implemented in the long run (cf. Beitz, *Political Theory*, p. 156).

Claim (b) raises however another, strategic issue as well. Hoffmann might hold that in the public forum one should emphasize intermediate objectives at the expense of one's long-term vision, because otherwise one might easily lose allies through disagreements over the feasibility or desirability of distant ideals. This conjecture finds some confirmation in his remark that Falk's ideal, though a suitable long-term objective, also harbors the danger of becoming "a splendid argument for doing nothing until we have a nice kind of world government" (p. 140). If that is a real danger, one might want to focus the attention of politicians on intermediate objectives, conceding—but only tactically, for the time being—that

> the first duty of the statesman is to his own community; he is not at the helm to abolish the race, although it is proper to ask him to make it more moderate and sportslike . . . the international competition . . . is here to stay" (pp. 34f., 204; see once more the passage quoted in note 10).

The third source of disagreement is then again more apparent than real in that the relevant considerations on balance tend to uphold the hope for a fruitful division of labor and collaboration between political science and political philosophy. Ideal theory will deepen and unify our commitments concerning social justice, but it must be complemented by suitable intermediate objectives so as not to discourage people into doing nothing at all. And the philosopher should take to heart two further points: The value of an ideal is not an all-or-nothing affair, does not hinge on its complete implementation—even small steps can make a tremendous difference in human terms. And, just as one might proceed toward an ideal along different routes, so different ideals may allow their adherents to agree about the first stretch of the road. If these last two points are stressed, then the introduction of philosophical ideals into the political arena need not at all lead to despair or to greater divisiveness.

Despite his harsh attacks, the essence of Hoffmann's assessments and proposals can then be accommodated within the new global liberalism, with which he already shares the commitment to liberal values (pp. 8f.). If both sides are willing to learn from one another, the political scientist's uplifted politics may very well converge with an applied ethics grounded in ideal theory.

II

Turning now to Terry Nardin's work, *Law, Morality, and the Relations of States*, I shall try to show that its main line of argument is unsuccessful, that its liberal appearance is deceptive, and that its conclusions are morally implausible. The discussion is meant to clarify the sense in which a just global order is best conceived as liberal.

Contrary to Hoffmann, Nardin offers a systematic account of global justice that focuses on major institutions. As the centerpiece of this account, he introduces a distinction between two different conceptions of association. *Purposive* association is arranged around some shared goal or vision of the good by appeal to which rules and practices can be given an (always provisional) instrumental justification. *Practical* association, on the other hand, is conceived as a *modus vivendi* or scheme of mutual accommodation, animated by the assumption that the members' ends and goals will be diverse and often incompatible. Here the operative rules and practices are viewed as indefeasible procedural devices and protections. Nardin's fundamental claim is that whereas legitimate purposive associations may be formed within (and according to the rules of) an enduring social system, that system itself must, if it is to be just, satisfy the conditions of practical association.

One conclusion Nardin wants to draw from this claim is that a (national or global) society committed to anything like Rawls's difference principle would be purposive and hence unjust.[9] In discussing economic arrangements, Nardin transforms his purposive/practical distinction into the question

> whether a just international order is one in which the conduct of states conforms to the common rules of international society, or one in which wealth and power are more evenly distributed. . . . The concept of distributive justice is tied to a purposive conception of society and government and has no place in discourse concerning practical association (pp. 256, 261).

At first it may seem that in presenting these disjuncts as mutually exclusive Nardin (like Hoffmann) overlooks the possibility of combining the two. In order to achieve greater equality of wealth and power, we need not abandon the commitment to practical association, to common rules—we may instead work toward a different model of practical association, one that would engender a more egalitarian distribution. And given the advantages, from a liberal point of view, of a procedural over a goal-based institutional scheme, this is precisely Rawls's strategy for domestic, and hence the Rawlsian strategy for international, society.

But Nardin has a response to this objection which, though not developed explicitly, operates throughout his book. The response is this: if our commitment to a particular set of practices is based on any substantive grounds, then it is these grounds rather than those practices which determine the character of our commitment. Thus, even if these practices are procedural (that is, do not permit appeal to any shared purposes), our commitment may still fall under the conception of purposive association if the practices themselves are thought to depend for their legitimacy on some ulterior principle (assessing, for example, alternative sets of practices in terms of their distributional effects). One reason is that some such principle, recognized as the ultimate court of appeal in matters of

9. Another main target of this attack is the United Nations because of its (purposive) commitment to social progress: to the promotion of human rights and of more equitable international practices and procedures (pp. 105ff.).

justice, would function like a shared purpose in that any set of practices could always be accepted only provisionally, subject to the possible claim that some alternative scheme does better by the principle in question.[10]

Now first of all, this defense does not license Nardin's rejection of *any* "international order . . . in which wealth and power are more evenly distributed," because such an order might consist of procedural practices whose legitimacy is not thought to rest on any further ground (such as their tendency to engender an egalitarian distribution).

More importantly, the defense has disastrous consequences for Nardin's account as a whole. In general terms the problem is that, if we are not to recognize any ulterior values or principles in terms of which to assess alternative sets of practices, then we are left with no grounds at all for preferring any one set of practices over any other. On Nardin's wonderfully paradoxical account of justice, we must pledge allegiance to a set of procedural practices for the adoption of which we do *not* have any substantive reasons. What reasons might possibly be available in support of that strange claim itself, of the demand for a model of "truly" practical association? Nardin can no longer adopt the traditional liberal gambit of appealing to the (morally) preferable effects of procedural practices in terms of freedom and pluralism, flexibility and efficiency, since all these values must now count as shared purposes, making purposive any model of association they are called upon to support.

In his attempt to offer reasons *other* than "purposes" for his central tenet, Nardin is thus reduced to some rather dubious a priori arguments. He contends, for example, that, since of all rules and practices only those of truly practical association are indefeasible or "authoritative," these must be accorded absolute primacy (pp. 11, 251). In analogy to the ontological proof for God's existence, this argument assumes what must be shown: namely that we *should* be committed to some model of truly

10. For Nardin the *same* procedural practices may exemplify either the purposive or the practical conception of association, depending on whether these practices are accepted (at least partly) for the sake of some (morally) desirable effects or without further substantive reasons at all. Rawls's advocacy of his basic liberties would therefore, contrary to Nardin (p. 262), make them, too, fall under the purposive conception, because any specific list of basic liberties is to be accepted only provisionally, subject to the possible claim that some alternative list would have greater worth in protecting and enhancing the freedom of the representative citizen (e.g., *Theory of Justice*, pp. 197ff.).

practical association, and thus recognize such authoritative rules, in the first place.[11]

A different conceptual argument asserts that "the purposive conception of international society is essentially an incoherent one," because "[t]he pursuit of shared purposes presupposes the availability of procedures according to which the agreement to cooperate in a common pursuit can be made" (pp. 6, 14; cf. also pp. 132, 154, 171). But this belief that persons cannot pursue a shared purpose when agreement procedures are unavailable is not only fantastic—it also undermines the whole point of Nardin's book by showing that all practices he rejects as purposive could only come about as legitimate understandings or joint ventures, agreed upon according to the rules of an underlying practical association. Moreover, in the emergence of at least some rules of truly practical association, such agreement in accordance with prior practices and rules must, on pain of infinite regress, be dispensable. And Nardin offers no reason why it should *always* be necessary for the emergence of all other practices— to the contrary, he says of practices in general that "they may emerge from habit and usage, like the principles of a cuisine handed down from one generation of cooks to the next" (p. 7).[12]

But even if the superiority of truly practical association were conceded, the same problem would recur. On Nardin's account there can be no grounds for preferring any one model of such association over any other, because the grounds for such a preference would count as common goals making the entire conception (model and grounds) purposive and hence

11. Along the same lines Nardin also claims that "evaluation of the common rules from the standpoint of their desirability presupposes acknowledgment of their authority [the duty to respond to the considerations embodied in them], for without this there are no rules whose desirability can be debated" (p. 265). Elsewhere we are told that, in view of its Latin roots, the word "justice" is "most at home" (p. 257) in discourse centering on Nardin's practical conception.

12. Michael Oakeshott, to whom Nardin repeatedly acknowledges his indebtedness, wisely foregoes the attempt to give reasons at this juncture. He simply asserts that something would not *be* a moral practice if our allegiance to it depended, even in part, on its (morally) desirable effects. See *On Human Conduct* (Oxford: The Clarendon Press, 1975), pp. 60–62. But even without Nardinian reasons the assertion remains suspect. It conveniently defines out of the moral debate the entire consequentialist tradition. And it does not square too well even with the remaining moral positions as is attested by Rawls's dictum: "All ethical doctrines worth our attention take consequences into account in judging rightness. One which did not would simply be irrational, crazy" (*Theory of Justice*, p. 30). In our pluralistic culture the Oakeshottian position, whatever its merits, can hardly disqualify all its competitors as not even understanding what "morality" ("justice") *means*.

unjust. Nardin accepts this consequence with one exception. Since some models would "permit the impartial application of arbitrary and discriminatory rules," he champions a narrower conception of practical association—one excluding rules and practices that do not treat all participants as formal equals (p. 258):

> the demand for justice is restricted to the demand for impartiality— that is, for the impartial application of rules that are themselves impartial in the sense that they reflect the liberty and formal equality of the members of the community (p. 265).

No reasons are offered for why liberty and formal equality should not count as shared purposes (in contrast to, say, the "right to a fair share"— p. 16); nor does Nardin take up the familiar and rather complicated problems concerning how "impartiality," "liberty," "formal equality," "arbitrary," and "discriminatory" are to be defined.

With respect to schemes falling under his narrower conception of practical association, Nardin holds that the participants in an ongoing scheme must honor the rules and practices presently in force. They are free to work for changes, but only insofar as the scheme permits: "any proposed alteration must itself be evaluated according to the constitutional principles embodied in international law and morality" (p. 270). This conservative stipulation—while it leaves open what one is to do when faced with an *unjust* scheme, that is, one that is either purposive or does not treat all its members as formal equals—does indeed seem plausible *if* one assumes that all models of (narrowly) practical association are equally just. But is this assumption itself plausible?

In response to that challenge, Nardin is concerned to reject the claim that global justice demands supranational institutions charged with the creation, enforcement, and authoritative determination of international law. He is hostile to such institutions and, while unable to condemn them as unjust (so long as they operate in a procedural manner and are not accepted for the sake of, say, their effectiveness), certainly considers them unnecessary. He argues at length that an international law emerging from custom, sporadically enforced through self-help, and interpreted by international lawyers and national officials, is still law—provided it evokes enough compliance so that it can be said to exist at all (pp. 126f., 132). Beyond that minimum, effectiveness is irrelevant to the the justice of a scheme. This Nardin *must* say, given his commitment to the perfect and equal justice of all models of narrowly practical association (which must never be altered in ways they don't themselves provide for). But how *can* justice be indifferent to considerations of effectiveness, how *can* it be always impermissible to overturn such schemes even if they barely work?

The implied equal justice of all models of practical association has two further unacceptable implications in the area of human rights. First, Nardin asserts that all these models treat *persons* as formal equals (p. 258). This however is not true—even ideally—if (as on Nardin's favorite model) persons form societies of formal equals which in turn form an international society of formally equal states. The equal rights of individuals may differ markedly from state to state, so that formal equality within each state plus formal equality among states need not amount to formal equality of persons worldwide. There is then a conflict between Nardin's claim that organizing humankind as a society of formally equal states is just, and his claim that justice demands the absence of arbitrary discrimination against persons (p. 258)—nationality is a main source of such discrimination today.

Secondly, Nardin's contention that international justice is achieved by *any* practical association of *states* implies that it "is not . . . a necessary feature of international law that it include provisions protecting the liberty of individuals within each state" (p. 53). To be sure, Nardin is clearly sympathetic to human rights. He emphasizes that certainly international law *can* contain such protections without violating formal equality among states (p. 275) and that it "has for some time been moving in the direction of setting minimum standards for the treatment of individuals by states" (p. 235). Yet the fact remains that Nardin's conception of justice is perfectly indifferent to the presence or absence of such protections—another, I submit, unacceptable implication.

Nardin's book displays systematic indifference to (and in some cases animosity toward) fundamental liberal convictions—to human rights, to roughly equal chances for political participation, to a greater diffusion of educational opportunities and material resources, and to the effective and uniform rule of law. Still, Nardin does endorse the central liberal thesis that any just global order would center on procedural rules and practices protecting the liberty and formal equality of every human being. However, not even this much can be derived from his account—which demonstrates once again how the quest for pristine neutrality can succeed only at the price of vacuity.

## III

The foregoing considerations have lent some support, I hope, to the program of developing a long-term liberal strategy for global institutional change. This program must satisfy Hoffmann's demand for "despecialization" (p. 227) by integrating political philosophy and social theory (economics, sociology, psychology, political science, history, and jurisprudence). The projected global institutional structure, featuring procedural practices supportive of personal autonomy, must be effective and able to maintain itself in our world under modern conditions. And it must be within reach from where we are, via a realistic transitional path not involving unacceptable moral costs. Developing a promising strategy in light of these demands requires a thorough understanding of social regularities and of the present international regime. Just as social science without moral vision is blind, a philosophical ideal undeveloped through social theory is empty.

    I would like to thank the Editors of *Philosophy & Public Affairs* and Charles Larmore for helpful comments and discussion. Work on this review essay was supported by a grant from the Columbia University Council for Research in the Humanities.

DONALD C. HUBIN          Of Bindings and By-products:
                        Elster on Rationality

Rationality is on the rise. Not as a property of people, of course, but as a subject of philosophical discussion. Long a favorite with philosophers, it is enjoying even greater popularity as battles are waged over whether it consists in the maximization of objective value or merely subjective value, or whether it requires maximization of anything at all, whether rationality in situations of risk requires acting on objective probabilities, subjective probabilities, or some other probabilities, how one should act when ignorant of the relevant probabilities, and whether such conditions of ignorance ever really obtain.

Into this battlefield Jon Elster introduces two salvos, *Ulysses and the Sirens* and *Sour Grapes*. These books take the reader on a sometimes dizzying tour of selected topics in economics, evolutionary theory, literature, sociology, historiography, and philosophy. In an age of overspecialization, these works are refreshingly interdisciplinary; they will entertain and educate people with widely varied backgrounds and interests. Perhaps they will even foster dialogue between students of diverse disciplines.

Because both books are collections of essays only loosely connected by various recurrent themes, it isn't feasible to give a complete summary of the contributions they make. Elster thinks that one significant contribution is providing a challenge to the received view of what an action is. He writes:

The following books are discussed in this review essay: Jon Elster, *Ulysses and the Sirens* (Cambridge: Cambridge University Press, 1979); Jon Elster, *Sour Grapes* (Cambridge: Cambridge University Press, 1983). Citations from the first will be indicated by *US* and those from the second by *SG*.

An action is the outcome of a choice within constraints. The choice, according to the orthodox view, embodies an element of freedom, the constraints one of necessity. In non-standard cases, however, these equations do not hold. The title of an earlier book on rational and irrational behavior, *Ulysses and the Sirens*, is a reminder that men are sometimes free to choose their own constraints. *Sour Grapes* conversely reflects the idea that the preferences underlying a choice may be shaped by constraints. Considered together, these two non-standard phenomena are sufficiently important to suggest that the orthodox theory is due for fundamental revision. (*SG*, p. vii)

The phenomena mentioned seem, *pace* Elster, to pose no real challenge to the orthodoxy he describes. But there is much more in the books than is reflected in this passage. And much of it is a challenge to orthodoxy—though the orthodoxy is that of the theory of rational action and not of action generally. For example, Elster argues that rationality is not a maximizing but a "satisficing" concept (*US*, pp. 133–37 and *SG*, pp. 2–26).[1] He claims, contra the Bayesians, that there are cases of decision under ignorance (*US*, pp. 128–33). He asserts that the standard decision-theoretic (parametric) conception of rationality is "strange or even contradictory" compared with strategic rationality (*US*, p. 117). And he takes steps toward developing and defending a conception of both individual and collective rationality that places substantive constraints on preferences and beliefs (*SG*, Chap. 1).

In what follows I shall, for the most part, avoid those aspects of Elster's work that question the received view of rational action. I shall focus instead on two issues that are recurrent topics in both of these books and that Elster believes have interesting implications for moral and political philosophy: precommitment and self-defeating pursuits. Precommitting, or binding, oneself is an indirect strategy for achieving an end; it can loosely be described as 'self-coercion'. Like other indirect strategies, it allows one to achieve an end that might otherwise be attainable only with difficulty, if at all—a sort of rational "tacking into the wind." Elster discusses self-defeating pursuits because, he believes, there are some states that resist even indirect rational strategies. Though they can be brought about by action, they cannot be brought about as the intended result of

1. He never, though, reconciles this claim with his position that humans, in contrast to animals and evolutionary processes are "globally *maximizing* machines" (*US*, pp. 9–18).

action. It may be possible to get "there" from "here," but not by trying. These states are, in Elster's terminology, "essentially by-products"; their pursuit is doomed to failure by the pursuit itself.

These two issues are of general interest because they concern the power and the limitations of rational strategies. They are of special interest to us because of the moral and political applications to which Elster puts them.

PRECOMMITMENT

Thomas Schelling has demonstrated the virtues of precommitment in strategic interaction.[2] By binding yourself—making certain courses of action impossible or very costly—you can manipulate an opponent or prevent him from manipulating you. If, for example, a union leader stakes his reputation on his refusal to approve a contract that includes a reduction in wages, he might thereby gain the upper hand in wage negotiations. Similarly, a government might adopt a firm policy of never paying ransom, making this a matter of principle, in order to deter extortionist threats. Such are the Orwellian oddities of strategic interaction: weakness can be strength.

In the title essay of *Ulysses and the Sirens*, Elster reminds us that strategy begins at home, for we may wish to manipulate (and avoid manipulation by) ourselves as much as others. More precisely, our present selves may wish to manipulate our future selves and to prevent our near future selves from manipulating our further future selves.

The strategy of precommitment is one very useful way of dealing with the practical problem of weakness of will. If you don't want to drink this weekend, lock up the liquor and put the key in the safe-deposit box until Monday.

Precommitment has other functions as well, largely ignored by Elster. It is not only our future irrationality we might wish to protect ourselves from, but our future rationality as well. Indeed, even the example that gives the book its title may not involve weakness of will. We are, I suppose, inclined to believe that the song of the Sirens would entice Ulysses to order his ship into the rocks without making it rational (either subjectively or objectively) for him to do so. But this may not be true. The story is

2. Thomas C. Schelling, *The Strategy of Conflict* (Cambridge, MA: Harvard University Press, 1960).

vague about the effect of the song of the Sirens. If it were to cause him to believe, falsely but reasonably, that steering into the rocks would not wreck his ship, his action may maximize his expected utility given his actual preferences and beliefs. If the song were to cause his preferences to change so that getting closer to the Sirens were the only thing important to Ulysses, his action may maximize his expected utility given his actual preferences and true beliefs. In either case, Ulysses may not be worried about weakness of will, but about the harm he will do quite rationally (either subjectively or objectively).

The further uses of precommitment only serve to make the strategy more interesting and an understanding of it more important. It is not as simple a concept as it might appear. But Elster offers a "tentative definition" (*US*, pp. 37–47) that is adequate for our purposes although problems remain.[3] Slightly paraphrased, his account is this:

An agent, A, binds (precommits) himself if:
  (i) A carries out a certain decision at time $t_1$ in order to increase the probability that A will carry out another decision at time $t_2$;
  (ii) the act at $t_1$ does not have the effect of inducing a change in the set of options that will be available at the later time in such a way that the new feasible set includes the old one;
  (iii) the effect of carrying out the decision at $t_1$ is to set up some causal process in the external world;
  (iv) the resistance against carrying out the decision at $t_1$ is smaller than the resistance that would have opposed the carrying out of the decision at $t_2$ had the decision at $t_1$ not intervened; and,
  (v) the act at $t_1$ is an act of commission, not omission.

Elster applies the concept of precommitment toward the understanding of Pascal's Wager, Descartes' critique of instant rationality, approaches to consistent planning, manipulation of people through endogenous preference changes, and the explanation of various historical and political phenomena. I shall focus on the last two applications because they are

3. For example, clause (i) would be better phrased as "A carries out a decision at $t_1$ in order to *decrease* the probability that he will carry out another decision he believes he may make later." Ulysses' actions while tied to the mast can hardly be termed a "carrying out" of his decision not to steer the ship into the rocks. To avoid practical vacuity, condition (iii) should be rephrased to require that the effect of carrying out the decision at $t_1$ on the probability of future actions is through an external causal mechanism. And neither clause (iv) nor (v) seems to be a necessary condition for precommitment.

most likely to be of interest to readers of this journal. What Elster has to say about these issues is interesting in its own right and, though I shall argue that neither manipulation through endogenous preference change nor the political phenomena that interest Elster are correctly analyzed as cases of precommitment, it is instructive to see why.

Take first his discussion of manipulation through endogenous preference change. It is obvious that our preferences often change in light of our experience and that our experience is influenced by our choices. In this way our choices may affect our preferences. This raises the possibility that a person who would not choose to go directly from $state_1$ to $state_3$, deeming the latter to be less valuable than the former, might nonetheless willingly go from $state_1$ to $state_3$ indirectly. This is because he may prefer some other state, $state_2$, to $state_1$ and move to it, and $state_2$ may influence his preferences in such a way that he comes to prefer $state_3$ to either alternative. One rather obvious example of this would be the case of a problem social drinker—Larry the Lush. Larry is, he regrets, sober. He would much prefer to have a slight buzz. However, he certainly does not want to get really drunk and embarrass himself as he has so often in the past. Unfortunately, he knows that once he has a few drinks to loosen up, he will want to get roaring drunk and have no concern for his self-respect.

This scenario raises the possibility of manipulation—of creating $state_2$ simply to lure another from $state_1$ to $state_3$. Someone who wishes to see Larry put the lampshade on his head and sing his out-of-key rendition of "Feelings" can offer him the first drink and let nature take its course.

Is such manipulation permissible? Elster thinks not. Indeed, he sees "no essential difference between" this sort of manipulation and coercion. "Coercion takes place," Elster says, "when an individual prefers $x$ over $y$, and continues to do so even when someone (physically) coerces him into doing $y$" (*US*, p. 82). This account is both unhelpful and counter-intuitive. The fact that Elster uses 'coerces' to define 'coercion' and does not analyze the former notion makes the analysis unilluminating. And it is an inaccurate account of our ordinary concept of coercion because most of us would consider some acts coercive even if the agent did not maintain his earlier preferences. Perhaps the clearest example of this is when a person is forced to kill himself. What Elster would say of this example, I don't know; of a more mundane example—one in which an agent comes to prefer the act he was coerced into doing—Elster says that the agent has been "seduced," not subjected to "coercion" (in his sense). "Seduction occurs when an individual initially prefers $x$ over $y$, but comes to prefer $y$ over $x$ once he has been coerced into doing $y$" (*US*, p. 82). This is even further from ordinary usage; but ordinary usage is not our concern here.

Elster finds both seduction and coercion to be intrinsically morally objectionable. Manipulation of a person through endogenous preference changes is, he thinks, conceptually distinct from either of these but morally on a par with them. He calls this kind of manipulation 'persuasion'. It occurs when "an individual is led by a sequence of short-term improvements into preferring $y$ over $x$, even if initially he preferred $x$ over $y$" (*US*, p. 83). Though this may appear to be merely a sequence of voluntary choices, Elster thinks this appearance hides a moral problem. Morally, "persuasion" is not at all like voluntary choice, which occurs when an "individual initially prefers $y$ over $x$, and does $y$ for that reason" (*US*, p. 82).

This issue is of great importance and interest. Elster's view suggests that government programs of inducement are just as morally objectionable as alternative coercive plans. He discusses at some length a plan suggested by C. C. von Weiszäcker to entice farmers away from the land and into the city by paying them to move. Once in the city, the hypothesis goes, the former farmers will come to prefer city life and the financial inducements can be dropped. A variety of other examples come to mind: meeting the gasoline shortage by subsidizing the purchase of small, fuel-efficient cars for a short period of time with the expectation that many will come to prefer such cars even without the subsidy; undermining consumer brand loyalty by offering free samples or below-cost discounts to lure potential customers into using one's product with the expectation that they will come to prefer it even at full price; using financial inducements to encourage one's children to work for good grades in the hope that once they become used to the self-satisfaction accompanying such success, that will be reward enough to sustain their efforts. Such "persuasions" seem common enough and not, in and of themselves, morally wrong.

Elster dissents. "My contention is that persuasion is more similar to seduction than to voluntary choice," he says (*US*, p. 83)—a claim that seems plausible until one remembers that by 'seduction' Elster means what most of us would call 'coercion'. He goes on to say that "there is no essential difference between coercion and seduction, nor between seduction and this form of persuasion" (*US*, p. 83). He concludes from this that Robert Nozick is wrong when he claims that inducements are never coercive.[4]

Because of the obvious importance of this and the initial implausibility of Elster's position, this claim merits persuasive argumentation (provided that is morally permissible). Unfortunately, it gets none. He contents himself with asserting that such persuasion is never justified unless you inform the object of it that you are about to manipulate him, because "[e]xploiting intrapsychic mechanisms that are unknown to the individual can never be justified" (*US*, p. 83). Though I take this literally to say that such actions are absolutely wrong, a more charitable (but, I think, equally false) interpretation of Elster takes the claim to assert merely that such actions are always *prima facie* wrong because of the manipulation involved. To establish even this weaker conclusion, Elster must show that the subsidies, discounts, and inducements suggested above are *prima facie* morally wrong. This seems not to be the case.

But let us ask what all of this about endogenous preference change has to do with precommitment. Elster believes that precommitment can take at least two forms. First, an agent can limit the set of feasible actions—more precisely, he can alter the world so that what might otherwise have been attractive and feasible becomes either unattractive, difficult, or impossible. Second, an agent may influence the mechanism by which he singles out a member of the feasible set of actions. This latter, Elster apparently believes, can be carried out either by deliberately bringing about a change in one's preferences or by refusing to allow such a change to take place. Hence, moving from $S_1$ to $S_2$ in order then to find $S_3$ attractive and move to it counts as precommitment. Similarly, refusing to move from $S_1$ to $S_2$ in order not to choose $S_3$ later counts as precommitment.

Both of these last two claims seem wrong. I do not question whether one can bind oneself by altering one's selection mechanism; to use Schelling's example, one might take a drug to make oneself irrational and avoid the possibility of being extorted—extortion threats being ineffective on

4. He ought not to put his point in this way since he does not deny the conceptual distinction between persuasion and coercion; even on his analysis of 'coercion' he is forced to agree with Nozick that the inducements in question are *not* coercive. Elster's point is really a normative one, disguised as a conceptual one.

an agent who is irrational in that particular way. But the cases Elster describes, though they are instances of self-conscious character management, are not cases of precommitment.[5]

In the first case, the agent chooses not to move from $S_1$ to $S_2$ for one of two reasons: either he fears that he will then voluntarily move to $S_3$— a prospect that he now dislikes—or he simply does not want to be the sort of person who prefers $S_3$ to other alternatives available. In either case, he has judged the desirability of $S_2$ to be less than that of remaining in $S_1$. In the first case it is the indirect effect of $S_2$ on his later states that bothers him; in the second case it is the effect of $S_2$ on his character to which he objects. If the agent fears that he might overlook or underweigh these subtle effects of $S_2$, he may well bind himself to prevent his moving to $S_2$ out of weakness of will. But the refusal to move to $S_2$ itself is not an act of precommitment for it does not render the move to $S_3$ more difficult or less desirable.

The second case is one in which the agent intentionally moves from $S_1$ to $S_2$ in order to make himself the sort of person who would prefer $S_3$ to the other two options. This is an odd case. Presumably, the agent does not prefer $S_3$ from the outset. If he did, there would be no need to move to $S_2$ in order to acquire this preference. (Perhaps he already prefers $S_3$ to the other options but doesn't have the strength of character to act on his preferences. If so, it might be that moving to $S_2$ would strengthen his resolve to move to $S_3$. But then this would not be a case of binding oneself to prevent the undesirable consequences of weakness of will; it would be a case of overcoming the weakness of will in the first place.) Thus, we are confronted with a case in which a person has a preference for a preference for $S_3$ but no preference for $S_3$. What are we to say of such a case? I think that we should follow Richard Jeffrey[6] and say that if a person moves to $S_2$ in order to have these preferences, then his preference for preferring $S_3$ was stronger than his preference for remaining out of $S_3$. If, on the other hand, he refuses to move to $S_2$, then his preference for staying out of $S_3$ was stronger than his preference for having the preference for $S_3$. In neither case should his action be seen as precom-

5. It is worth noting that neither case appears to fit Elster's own explicit, if provisional, account of 'precommitment'.

6. Richard C. Jeffrey, "Preference among Preferences," *Journal of Philosophy* 71 (1974):377–91. A revised version appears in *The Logic of Decision*, 2d ed. (Chicago: University of Chicago Press, 1983), pp. 214-27.

mitment. Again, this is because it is not a case of an agent manipulating his choice situation or his deliberative capacities to make a decision that would otherwise be possible or desirable not be so.

The two cases offered by Elster seem to be cases of precommitment only if we view an agent's preferences as binding him. But, of course, preferences do not generally bind an agent, even when they determine his action. The entire issue of endogenous preference change has no special relevance to the notion of precommitment.

The second of Elster's applications of the concept of precommitment that I will discuss here is that of a democracy binding itself through its constitution. There is no doubt that the populace of a democracy may be constrained by its constitution. At least two problems arise, however, when one attempts to interpret these constraints as arising from acts of precommitment. The first is pointed out by Elster and is, in fact, one of his recurrent themes: one cannot infer from the fact that some structure has an effect—even a desirable one—that it was designed in order to produce that effect. The second is that it is quite unclear that there is a single agent binding itself through an external mechanism as is required by the concept of precommitment. Since we may assume that constitutional constraints *are* designed to limit the actions of the majority in a democracy, the second problem is more serious.

Precommitment requires that there be a single agent who performs an action at one time with the intention of constraining itself at a later time. It is not at all clear that the act of imposing constitutional constraints will fit this model—especially in the case of intergenerational constraints.

Perhaps we can treat the agent as a population over time having the intention to bind itself. The problems with this approach are great and readily apparent. Even if they are overcome, this understanding of the agent would not allow the case of constitutional constraints to fit Elster's analysis. This is because the binding would then not be effected through an external causal mechanism. Instead, it would be analogous to a private side bet, which Elster intends the third clause of his definition to rule out as an instance of precommitment. Our single agent has, in effect, an agreement with itself not to undertake certain action without more than a majority vote. If, being convinced of the virtue of absolute pacifism but fearful of our own atavistic tendencies, we were to beat our swords into plowshares in order to prevent ourselves from retaliating for an attack, this might plausibly be seen as social precommitment. But if we merely promise ourselves that we won't do something that is in our power to do, we have not bound ourselves in the relevant sense.

It seems premature, then, to conclude with Elster that "the analysis of democracy has offered some convincing examples of political precommitment" (*US*, p. 103). It thus seems premature to conclude that the analysis of precommitment can give us a tool for understanding the constitutional constraints of a democracy.

## SELF-DEFEATING PURSUITS

Precommitment is an indirect strategy for achieving an end. It is often reasonable to employ it when a direct approach is less certain or more costly. There are other sorts of indirect strategies—for example, altering one's character in order to affect one's future choices. Taken together, indirect strategies provide a powerful, and often overlooked, technique for achieving our ends.

But the technique can also be overestimated. Elster's discussion of precommitment and the employment of indirect strategies for achieving one's ends in *Ulysses and the Sirens* leaves one with the impression that virtually any effect that can be brought about by human action can be brought about intentionally, either directly or indirectly.

This is a misconception, Elster believes, and he sets about to correct it in *Sour Grapes*. There are, he claims, states that are essentially by-products—that is, roughly, states that can be produced by action but cannot be produced as the intended effect of the action. When pursued, such states recede; they are attainable only by one who does not seek them. Failure to appreciate this fact leads to two related fallacies: the moral fallacy of by-products and the intellectual fallacy of by-products. The first occurs when one tries to bring about a state that is essentially a by-product—the second, when one attempts to explain such a state by reference to an agent's intention to bring it about.

Elster discusses at some length "willing what cannot be willed" or, less paradoxically, willing what cannot be brought about by a mere act of will. Examples discussed by Elster include being natural, sleeping, and forgetting. (Insomniacs will find his phenomenology of insomnia particularly interesting.) He sums up the discussion as follows: "[T]he absence of consciousness of something cannot be brought about by an act of consciousness, since this privative state is essentially a by-product" (*SG*, p. 50).

But this seems to be the wrong summation. Though most of us cannot bring about the states with which Elster is concerned merely by willing them, we can surely bring them about by "an act of consciousness." The point is especially clear if one considers sleep and forgetfulness. There are any number of conscious acts one can perform to induce these states. For inducing sleep, warm milk, hot baths, sex, a glass of wine, a few sleeping pills, or a beginning logic lecture have been known to do the trick. For forgetfulness, getting involved in an attention-consuming activity, sex, a few glasses of wine, or the sleeping pills again, can accomplish the end.

Elster's point cannot be that there are some states of ourselves that we cannot bring about *at* will. This is too mundane to mention. If his point is that there are states of ourselves that, by their very essence, cannot be brought about by design, it is an exciting and bold hypothesis. Unfortunately, it achieves its excitement and bravado by its appearance of blatant falsity.

Elster does nothing to reduce this appearance—not that he doesn't *try*. He offers three "responses." "First, even if a certain state can be achieved by indirect means, it may still be a fallacy to believe it can be achieved at will" (*SG*, p. 56). It certainly may be false to believe this, and it would be a fallacy to infer it from the fact that the state could be achieved indirectly. But is is an easy trick to point out fallacies that no one is tempted to commit. We should not allow this intellectual sleight of hand to distract our attention from the fact that Elster's remark is no reply to the objection that has been made.

Second, Elster says, "[e]ven assuming the technical feasibility of bringing about the states in question by indirect means, there may be a cost-benefit problem that stops us from doing so. Not everything that is technically possible is also economically rational" (*SG*, p. 56). True, but irrelevant. Elster's thesis is not that there are some states that, even if desirable, ought not to be brought about even by indirect means. No one disputes this. His claim is that there are some states that, "for conceptual and not only for empirical reasons," *cannot* be brought about both intentionally and intelligently. His second point does nothing to support this claim.

Finally, Elster claims he will argue, "There are states which resist the indirect as well as the direct attempts to bring them about" (*SG*, p. 57). 'Resist' is a crucial word here. For Elster's purposes, it must mean 'cannot be effected by'. But Elster argues no such thing. Instead, he gives a couple of examples of difficulties that might arise in employing certain indirect means to produce certain states that, he claims, are essentially by-products. The most memorable is the "hammock problem." Rocking oneself to sleep in a hammock may be impossible for some because just before one falls asleep, one has become too sleepy to continue the rocking. As the rocking stops, one awakens enough to resume the rocking—again, almost to the point of sleep.

For Elster's thesis to be true, there must be some states that we cannot produce intelligently and intentionally by *any* technology. (This is Elster's revised account of a state that is essentially a by-product.) To generalize from the problem of rocking oneself to sleep in a hammock would be rather hasty—all the more so since the state in question, sleep, is clearly attainable by indirect means. So much for Elster's arguments. What about his thesis?

Setting aside trivial cases, Elster's thesis seems doomed to falsity. All the states considered by Elster are, presumably, achievable in principle by sufficiently sophisticated methods of psychosurgery—methods that may be used to produce the state both intentionally and intelligently. Let us proceed even further into science fiction long enough to imagine a brain-state replicator. It works like this: if I desire to have the same brain state as another, I place the cap of the replicator on my head and aim the pick up at the person currently in the desired brain state. That state is instantly replicated in me. With such a technology at our disposal, there seems to be no brain state inherently beyond our ability to produce intentionally and intelligently.

If we had to rely on such science-fiction examples to refute Elster, this would show something interesting about the limitations on the indirect strategies available to us. It would not, though, support Elster's thesis, which takes seriously the notion of a state being *essentially* a by-product. And although I think that my brain-state replicator example is convenient in that it handles Elster's examples in one fell swoop, I don't regard such far-fetched examples as necessary. I see no reason to believe that even without such exotic technology there are some states that cannot be produced except as by-products.

If we have no good reason to believe that there are such states, then most of what Elster says in his essay on by-products is unduly pessimistic. By employing indirect strategies, we can achieve far more than Elster concedes. And, more interestingly, the only political application to which Elster puts this thesis seems unwarranted. Let us turn finally to this issue.

Some have claimed that one of the main purposes of certain participatory political institutions is their educative function for those who are involved in them. Elster objects. "This would be to turn into the main purpose of politics something that can only be a by-product" (SG, p. 91). Although he has not argued that the enlightenment in question *is* essentially a by-product, it may still be true that if political institutions are created with the aim of producing greater awareness in the participants, they cannot achieve this.

Elster's real concern is whether it is possible to achieve this aim if one makes it the *public* justification of the institution. Some, like Kant and Rawls, insist that an aim can justify an institution only if making that aim the public justification of that institution is consistent with achieving that aim. If they are correct, then those aims the publication of which would preclude their attainment could not serve as the justification of political institutions.

Elster believes that if I involve myself in a political process with self-development being my sole or primary aim, I am sure to fail. This is because the end I have in mind is essentially a by-product and hence cannot be produced both intelligently and intentionally. For argument's sake, let us grant him this. He concludes from this that the achievement of such states cannot be the public justification of the political institutions. Herein lies the fallacy.

There are at least two lacunae in the inference. The first is in his assumption that the public justification of an institution must be the aim of individuals in setting up the institution. This need not be so. Each individual may strive to set up an institution for purposes of pure economic self-interest. But each may recognize that this sort of consideration does not constitute a satisfactory public moral justification of the institution. Each may then search for some effect of the institution that would serve this function. They may find it in the institution's ability to promote personal development or class consciousness. Each takes this to be the public moral justification of the institution, but no one establishes the institution with this as his aim.

The second flaw in the argument is more interesting for our present purposes. In order to see this fault clearly, let us grant Elster what we challenged above: that if there is an aim that justifies a political institution, then those who set up the institution do so in order to achieve this aim. The argument is fallacious, even allowing this, because Elster confounds two different aims. He fails to distinguish our aim in establishing an institution from our aim in participating in that institution. But these are quite distinct concepts and often distinct aims. One can imagine, for example, a follower of Adam Smith promoting the free market for the sole reason that it maximizes overall efficiency. Nevertheless, his reason for participating in the market once established is, of course, quite different. Given this crucial distinction, there seems to be no reason why some aim like personal development or class consciousness cannot be the public justification of an institution and the only aim of those who establish that institution and still be achieved by the institution. The motivation for participating in the institution need not be the same as that for establishing it.

This last point suggests an idea that should not have been lost on anyone as fascinated with precommitment as Elster is: one can create political institutions so as to bind oneself to become involved and achieve personal development. We might imagine members of a society that is subject to a benign dictator who choose to bind themselves to political action by establishing a democracy. Once it is established, self-interest may provide sufficient motivation to participate fully. The public justification of the institution is personal development, as is the aim of the populace in establishing it. Once established, the people do not aim at such development. Indeed, they may rue the day they forced themselves to achieve it, even as Ulysses regretted (for a time) his order to be bound to the mast. Their motivation for participation is of quite a different sort. Hence, they can achieve personal growth even if this growth cannot be achieved by a person who participates for the purpose of achieving it.

Surprisingly, Elster has underestimated the power of precommitment. "Where there's a will, there's a way," is surely false—but not for conceptual reasons. The interesting limitations on what can be achieved rationally are empirical.

For helpful discussions of issues I have focused on in this article, I am indebted to Brad Armendt, Daniel M. Farrell, Robert Kraut, and George Schumm. My debt to Daniel Farrell extends beyond this; his careful reading of an earlier draft of this paper has done much to improve it. I am also grateful to the Editors of *Philosophy & Public Affairs* for many helpful suggestions.

## Subscription Rates

U.S. and Canadian Subscribers
Individuals:
$14.50 per year
$24.00 for two years
$34.00 for three years
Institutions: $22.50 per year
Student Rate: $ 9.00 per year
Single Issues: $ 5.00
*Special rates for classroom use*

All Other Subscribers
Individuals:
$18.25 per year
$30.00 for two years
$42.50 for three years
Institutions: $28.00 per year
Student Rate: $11.00 per year
Single Issues: $ 6.25
*Please add $3.50 per year for postage and handling.*

To subscribe, write to:
Princeton University Press
Box PPA
3175 Princeton Pike
Lawrenceville, NJ 08648

## Advertisements

Inquiries should be directed to
Journals Advertising Manager
Princeton University Press
41 William Street
Princeton, NJ 08540

*Philosophy & Public Affairs*
acknowledges the assistance
given to the Editor by the
University of Southern
California.

## Notes for Contributors

Contributions should be typewritten and
double-spaced on standard-weight paper.
Footnotes should also be double-spaced,
numbered consecutively, and gathered at
the end. Two clear photocopies should be
submitted. Submissions will not be
returned unless accompanied by a stamped,
self-addressed envelope. Manuscripts and
related correspondence should be directed
to the Managing Editor, *Philosophy &
Public Affairs*, Princeton University Press,
41 William Street, Princeton, NJ 08540.

Books for review and correspondence
concerning the Review Section should be
directed to Professor Charles Beitz,
Department of Political Science,
Swarthmore College, Swarthmore, PA
19081.

## Photocopying

Authorization to photocopy items for
internal or personal use, or the internal or
personal use of specific clients, is granted
by Princeton University Press for libraries
and other users registered with the
Copyright Clearance Center (CCC)
Transactional Reporting Service, provided
that a base fee of $00.00 per copy, plus
$0.05 per page is paid directly to CCC, 21
Congress Street, Salem, MA 01970, for
copying beyond that permitted by Sections
107 and 108 of the United States Copyright
Law. This consent does not extend to other
kinds of copying, such as copying for
general distribution, for advertising or
promotional purposes, for creating new
collective works, or for resale.
0048-3915/86 $0.00 + .05

Bulk rates for photocopying for classroom
use are available on a sliding scale from the
Managing Editor, *Philosophy & Public
Affairs*, Princeton University Press, 41
William Street, Princeton, NJ 08540.

# Philosophy & Public Affairs

**PRINCETON UNIVERSITY PRESS**
Box PPA
3175 Princeton Pike
Lawrenceville, New Jersey 08648

. . . . . . . . . . . . . . . . . . . . . . . . . . . . . . . . . . . . . . . . . . . . . . . . . . . . .

Enter my subscription to **Philosophy & Public Affairs**
@ $ _____ for _____ year(s).
Payment must be enclosed with order. Please do not send cash.
U.S. and Canadian Subscribers
*Individuals:* $14.50 per year/$24.00 two years/$34.00 three years
*Institutions:* $22.50 per year  *Student rate:* $9.00 per year
All Other Subscribers (please add $3.50 per year postage & handling)
*Individuals:* $18.25 per year/$30.00 two years/$42.50 three years
*Institutions:* $28.00 per year  *Student rate:* $11.00 per year

Name _____

Address _____

City_____ State _____ Zip _____

Field or Discipline _____

. . . . . . . . . . . . . . . . . . . . . . . . . . . . . . . . . . . . . . . . . . . . . . . . . . . . .

# Philosophy & Public Affairs

**PRINCETON UNIVERSITY PRESS**
Box PPA
3175 Princeton Pike
Lawrenceville, New Jersey 08648

. . . . . . . . . . . . . . . . . . . . . . . . . . . . . . . . . . . . . . . . . . . . . . . . . . . . .

Enter my subscription to **Philosophy & Public Affairs**
@ $ _____ for _____ year(s).
Payment must be enclosed with order. Please do not send cash.
U.S. and Canadian Subscribers
*Individuals:* $14.50 per year/$24.00 two years/$34.00 three years
*Institutions:* $22.50 per year  *Student rate:* $9.00 per year
All Other Subscribers (please add $3.50 per year postage & handling)
*Individuals:* $18.25 per year/$30.00 two years/$42.50 three years
*Institutions:* $28.00 per year  *Student rate:* $11.00 per year

Name _____

Address _____

City_____ State _____ Zip _____

Field or Discipline _____

. . . . . . . . . . . . . . . . . . . . . . . . . . . . . . . . . . . . . . . . . . . . . . . . . . . . .

# Business & Professional Ethics Journal

Published quarterly, this journal provides a forum for the discussion
and analysis of ethical issues
associated with business enterprises and the professions

## EDITORS

Robert J. Baum, Norman E. Bowie, Deborah G. Johnson

### EDITORIAL ADVISORY BOARD

## PAPERS PUBLISHED INCLUDE

*Ethical Responsibilities of Engineers in Large Organizations:*     Richard T. De George
*The Pinto Case*     University of Kansas
Commentary     Hart T. Mankin, Vice President, Columbia Gas System

*Privacy, Polygraphs and Work*     George G. Brenkert, University of Tennessee
Commentary . David Linowes, formerly Chairman, U.S. Privacy Protection Commission

*What is Hamlet to McDonnell-Douglas or*     Peter A. French
*McDonnell-Douglas to Hamlet: DC-10*     Trinity University
Commentary     Homer Sewell, formerly Director, Boeing Corporation

*Lawgiving for Professional Life*     Lisa H. Newton, Fairfield University
Commentary     Donald E. Wilson, Vice President, Michael Baker Company

*Licensing Professions: Preliminary Considerations*     Bernard Gert, Dartmouth College
Commentary Donald Weinert, P.E., Exec. Director, National Society of Prof. Engineers

*Engineers Who Kill: Professional Ethics and the Paramountcy of*     Kenneth Kipnis
*Public Safety*     University of Hawaii
Commentary     James F. Fairman, Esq., Partner, Fairman, Frisk, Monaco

*The Sealed-Beam Case: Engineering in the Public and*     George P. E. Meese
*Private Interest*     Michigan Technological University
Commentary     Robert Knoll, Consumer's Union

*Ethical Issues in Plant Relocation*     John P. Kavanagh, University of Delaware
Commentary     Elmer W. Johnson, Senior Partner, Kirkland & Ellis

*The Ideological Use of Professional Codes*     John Kultgen, Univ. of Missouri-Columbia
Commentary Robin Alexander-Smith, Chief Counsel, Ethics, American Bar Association

*Conflict of Interest*     Michael Davis, Illinois State University
Commentary     William Snead, Attorney at Law, Superior Oil Company

## NEWS AND NOTES

Announcements of conferences, workshops and other opportunities for persons
interested in ethical issues in business and the professions.

## BOOK REVIEWS

Subscriptions: $15 to individuals, $30 to institutions for four issues per year. Foreign postage and handling (incl.
Canada) add $2.50 per year. Address: Business and Professional Ethics Journal, Subscription Office, Science and
Technology Studies Division, Rensselaer Polytechnic Institute, Troy, New York 12181

Philosophy
&Public
Affairs

# A MESSAGE TO INSTRUCTORS
# IN ETHICS AND SOCIAL AND
# POLITICAL PHILOSOPHY

Introduce your students to *Philosophy & Public Affairs* so that they may have the benefit of thoughtful, philosophically inclined viewpoints on current issues written by lawyers, political scientists, economists, and sociologists. Your students may receive this journal at a *special reduced rate of $9.00 (prepaid) for one year. With a minimum order of 10 prepaid subscriptions we'll include a complimentary instructor's subscription.

Box JB
*Philosophy & Public Affairs*        *Please enclose check or money*
41 William Street                    *order with coupon.*
Princeton, New Jersey 08540

☐ Enclosed is $_____ for _____ special student subscriptions.
☐ Ten or more orders are enclosed. Please include my
   complimentary subscription.
Begin subscriptions with the following issue:
☐ January  ☐ April  ☐ July  ☐ October

Professor: _____

College/University: _____

Address: _____

_____ Zip _____

*(Offer expires December 31, 1986)*

*This offer applies in U.S. and Canada only.

# DIALOGUE

## Canadian Philosophical Review/Revue canadienne de philosophie
### Vol. XXIII, No. 4, December/décembre 1984

**Rédacteur francophone:** François Duchesneau, Département de philosophie, Université de Montréal, C.P. 6128, succ. A, Montréal, Québec H3C 3J7

**English-language editor:** Michael McDonald, Department of Philosophy, University of Waterloo, Waterloo, Ontario N2L 3G1

# Philosophia

## Philosophical Quarterly of Israel
### Editor: Asa Kasher
### Vol. 15, Nos. 1-2

PHILOSOPHIA, Department of Philosophy, Bar-Ilan University, Ramat-Gan, 52100, Israel.

# Philosophy and Rhetoric

Editor: Donald Phillip Verene
Associate Editor: Gerard A. Hauser
Book Review Editor: Christopher Lyle Johnstone

Annual subscription rates: U.S.A., $16.50 (individual), $22.50 (institutional). All other, $20.00 (individual), $26.00 (institutional)
Published by: The Pennsylvania State University Press, 215 Wagner Building, University Park, PA 16802. Editorial Office: Department of Philosophy, Emory University, Atlanta, GA 30322

# REVUE INTERNATIONALE DE PHILOSOPHIE

*Editor*: Michel MEYER

143, av. A. Buyl, 1050 Brussels, Belgium

Each number is devoted to a particular movement, a particular philosopher, or a particular problem.

We publish 3 issues annually. Articles are written in English, French, German, or Italian.

Coming numbers:

Sartre, Common Sense
Bacon
Berkeley
Platon

Our last issue was devoted to *Herméneutique et néo-structuralisme*

(articles by H.-G. Gadamer, J. Derrida, M. Frank, H. Birus and R. Schacht)

# social research

AN INTERNATIONAL QUARTERLY
OF THE SOCIAL SCIENCES

VOLUME 52, NUMBER 3
AUTUMN 1985

*A publication of the*
GRADUATE FACULTY
NEW SCHOOL FOR
SOCIAL RESEARCH

# BIOETHICS

Guest Editor
Arthur L. Caplan

Individual Subscriptions: $20; Institutions: $40.
Single copies available on request.
Editorial and Business Office:
66 West 12th Street, New York, N.Y. 10011
Room GF354

# PHILOSOPHY & SOCIAL CRITICISM

International Quarterly Journal / Volume 10, 1984, No. 3-4

## PHILOSOPHY & THE NUCLEAR DEBATE
*A Special Double Issue $5.95*

## ON THE EXTINCTION THESIS
*Ronald E. Santoni / Richard Routley*

## NUCLEAR WEAPONS, POWER & DOMINATION
*Louis Rene Beres / Michael W. Howard / Lyle V. Anderson / Clark Butler*

## ON NUCLEAR WEAPONS
*David Weinberger / Lawrence Kilbourne*

## THE MORALITY OF DETERRENCE
*George Hampsch / Rose Mary Volbrecht / Joseph C. Kunkel / Douglas P. Lackey / Duane L. Cady / John Donaghy*

*David M. Rasmussen, Editor*
*William C. Gay, Guest Editor*

*Subscription Rates $12 Student / $16 Individual / $46 Institutions / $3.95 Single Issues / $5.95 Double Issues / Send check or money order to PHILOSOPHY & SOCIAL CRITICISM , Department of Philosophy, Boston College, Chestnut Hill, MA 02167 USA*